Practice and homework

Year 6

This book is not photocopiable.

Rising Stars UK Ltd., 7 Hatchers Mews, Bermondsey Street,
London SE1 3GS

www.risingstars-uk.com

Every effort has been made to trace copyright holders and obtain their permission for the use of copyright materials. The author and publisher will gladly receive information enabling them to rectify any error or omission in subsequent editions.

All facts are correct at time of going to press.

First published as *New Framework Maths Practice and Homework Year 6*.
This reissue published 2011.
Text, design and layout © Rising Stars UK Ltd.

Cover design: Richard Scott
Design and illustration: Redmoor Design, Tavistock, Devon
Editorial consultant: Ann Todd

All rights reserved. No part of this publication may be reproduced, stored in a retrieval system, or transmitted, in any form by any means, electronic, mechanical, photocopying, recording or otherwise, without the prior permission of Rising Stars.

British Library Cataloguing in Publication Data
A CIP record for this book is available from the British Library.

ISBN: 978-1-84680-946-0

Printed by Craft Print International Ltd., Singapore

Contents

Coverage of Primary Framework for mathematics	4
How to use this book	6
Negative numbers	8
Square numbers	9
Factors and prime numbers	10
Fractions	11
Finding fractions of numbers and quantities	12
Fractions and decimals	13
Fractions, decimals and percentages	14
Multiplication – grid and partitioning methods	15
Division – using multiples of the divider	16
Division – short and long division	17
Understanding multiplication and division	18
Using a calculator	19
Checking results of calculations	20
Length, mass and capacity – reading scales 1	22
Length, mass and capacity – reading scales 2	24
Perimeter	26
Area	28
Time	30
2D shapes	32
Properties of 3D shapes	34
Position and direction	36
Angles	38
Angles in circles, triangles and straight lines	40
Multi-step problems	42
Shopping problems	43
Converting foreign currency	44
Calculating fractions and percentages	46
Problems involving length	48
Problems involving mass	50
Problems involving capacity	51
Problems involving imperial measures	52
Problems involving time	54
Frequency bar charts	56
Line graphs	58
Probability	60
Finding the mean and the median	62
Finding the mode	63
Finding the range	64

Coverage of Primary Framework for mathematics

	Page number
Using and applying mathematics	
Solve multi-step problems, and problems involving fractions, decimals and percentages; choose and use appropriate calculation strategies at each stage, including calculator use	14, 19, 20, 21, 30, 31, 42, 43, 48, 49, 50, 51, 52, 53, 54, 55
Tabulate systematically the information in a problem or puzzle; identify and record the steps or calculations needed to solve it, using symbols where appropriate; interpret solutions in the original context and check their accuracy	44, 45
Suggest, plan and develop lines of enquiry; collect, organise and represent information, interpret results and review methods; identify and answer related questions	46, 47
Represent and interpret sequences, patterns and relationships involving numbers and shapes; suggest and test hypotheses; construct and use simple expressions and formulae in words then symbols (e.g. the cost of c pens at 15 pence each is $15c$ pence)	
Explain reasoning and conclusions, using words, symbols or diagrams as appropriate	42, 43
Counting and understanding number	
Find the difference between a positive and a negative integer, or two negative integers, in context	8
Use decimal notation for tenths, hundredths and thousandths, partition, round and order decimals with up to three places, and position them on the number line	
Express a larger whole number as a fraction of a smaller one (e.g. recognise that 8 slices of a 5-slice pizza represents $8/5$ or $1 3/5$ pizzas); simplify fractions by cancelling common factors; order a set of fractions by converting them to fractions with a common denominator	11, 12, 13
Express one quantity as a percentage of another (e.g. express £400 as a percentage of £1000); find equivalent percentages, decimals and fractions	11
Solve simple problems involving direct proportion by scaling quantities up or down	
Knowing and using number facts	
Use knowledge of place value and multiplication facts to 10×10 to derive related multiplication and division facts involving decimals (e.g. 0.8×7, $4.8 \div 6$)	9
Use knowledge of multiplication facts to derive quickly squares of numbers to 12×12 and the corresponding squares of multiples of 10	9
Recognise that prime numbers have only two factors and identify prime numbers less than 100; find the prime factors of two-digit whole numbers	10
Use approximations, inverse operations and tests of divisibility to estimate and check results	15

COVERAGE OF PRIMARY FRAMEWORK FOR MATHEMATICS

	Page number
Calculating	
Calculate mentally with integers and decimals: U.t ± U.t, TU × U, TU ÷ U, U.t × U, U.t ÷ U	
Use efficient written methods to add and subtract integers and decimals, to multiply and divide integers and decimals by a one-digit integer, and to multiply two-digit and three-digit integers by a two-digit integer	15, 16, 17, 18
Relate fractions to multiplication and division (e.g. 6 ÷ 2 = ½ of 6 = 6 × ½); express a quotient as a fraction or decimal (e.g. 67 ÷ 5 = 13.4 or 13⅖); find fractions and percentages of whole-number quantities (e.g. ⅝ of 96, 65% of £260)	14, 46, 47
Use a calculator to solve problems involving multi-step calculations	
Understanding shape	
Describe, identify and visualise parallel and perpendicular edges or faces; use these properties to classify 2D shapes and 3D solids	32, 33, 34, 35
Make and draw shapes with increasing accuracy and apply knowledge of their properties	32, 33, 34, 35
Visualise and draw on grids of different types where a shape will be after reflection, after translations, or after rotation through 90° or 180° about its centre or one of its vertices	37
Use coordinates in the first quadrant to draw, locate and complete shapes that meet given properties	36, 37
Estimate angles, and use a protractor to measure and draw them, on their own and in shapes; calculate angles in a triangle or around a point	38, 39, 40, 41
Measuring	
Select and use standard metric units of measure and convert between units using decimals to two places (e.g. change 2.75 litres to 2750 ml, or vice versa)	24, 25
Read and interpret scales on a range of measuring instruments, recognising that the measurement made is approximate and recording results to a required degree of accuracy; compare readings on different scales, for example when using different instruments	22, 23
Calculate the perimeter and area of rectilinear shapes; estimate the area of an irregular shape by counting squares	26, 27, 28, 29
Handling data	
Describe and predict outcomes from data using the language of chance or likelihood	60, 61
Solve problems by collecting, selecting, processing, presenting and interpreting data, using ICT where appropriate; draw conclusions and identify further questions to ask	
Construct and interpret frequency tables, bar charts with grouped discrete data, and line graphs; interpret pie charts	56, 57, 58, 59
Describe and interpret results and solutions to problems using the mode, range, median and mean	8, 62, 63, 64

How to use this book

New Medal Maths has been created to provide you with lots of practice to support your maths learning.

To make it more fun for you, the activities are organised around an Olympic Games theme including sporting topics, training tips and the bronze, silver and gold medals. The medals indicate three different levels of difficulty.

As Pierre de Coubertin, the founder of the Modern Olympic Games, said "The most important thing in the Olympic Games is not to win but to take part …"!

Practice and more practice is the best method for getting results and improving your performance in maths.

For the best results:

a) read the explanation;

b) complete the questions at the most appropriate level;

c) use the hints and tips to help you;

d) see if you can complete the next level of questions!

Explanations
Explanations and examples are given to support you working independently.

Bronze Medal Questions
These questions are an ideal starting point. They support the work covered in the Silver questions.

Silver Medal Questions
These questions are set at the expected level for Year 6 as presented by the Primary Framework.

HOW TO USE THIS BOOK

Primary Framework for mathematics
Every objective is covered through an explanation, three levels of questions and hints and tips.

NUMBER AND ALGEBRA

Fractions, decimals and percentages

Use these facts to help you answer the questions.

Fractions, decimals and percentages facts

One whole = 100% $1\% = 0.01 = \frac{1}{100}$
One half = 50% $10\% = 0.1 = \frac{1}{10}$
One quarter = 25% $20\% = 0.2 = \frac{1}{5}$
One tenth = 10% $25\% = 0.25 = \frac{1}{4}$
                    $50\% = 0.5 = \frac{1}{2}$
                    $57\% = 0.57 = \frac{57}{100}$
                    $75\% = 0.75 = \frac{3}{4}$

Using a calculator
You can find difficult percentages by using a calculator. Look at this question.
526 football fans were asked who their favourite player was. 290 said David Beckham. What percentage said David Beckham was their favourite player?
Use a calculator
Key in '290' then 'divide symbol' then '526' then '%'. You should have 55.133. Round this answer down to 55%.

 Bronze

a) Try these questions without using a calculator:
1. What is 10% of 4 metres?
2. What is 75% of £100?
3. 25% of the people on the bus are wearing glasses. What percentage is not wearing glasses?
4. Dave got 30 out of 60 in his spelling test. Davina scored 35%. Who did better in the test – Dave or Davina?

b) Find these percentages by using halving and quartering.
1. 25% of £200
2. 50% of £260
3. 75% of £400
4. 25% of £280

 Silver

a) What percentages are equivalent to these decimals?
1. 0.41   2. 0.78

b) Try these without using a calculator:
1. Find 60% of £60
2. Find 70% of 300kg
3. A pair of trainers cost £45. It has a 10% discount in a sale. What is the sale price of the trainers?

c) Find these percentages by halving and quartering:
1. 12.5% of £48 000
2. 6.25% of 12 m

 Gold

Answer these questions using a calculator. Round the answers up or down.

a) Here are some Maths Test scores. What are their percentages?
1. Ben – 139 out of 146
2. Tanya – 141 out of 146
3. Andrea – 125 out of 146

b) How many out of 146 did each of these children score?
1. Leo – 85%
2. Finley – 92%
3. Jamie – 89%
4. Bruce – 67%
5. Alexa – 99%

 Training Tips
• To find 1% of something, first find 10% then find 10% of THAT answer. You can work out any percentage by adding all the 10%, 5% and 1% answers together!

Gold Medal Questions
These questions are a bit harder. They extend the work of the Silver questions.

Questions
There are hundreds of questions covering all the content for the Primary Framework.

Hints and Tips
Hints and tips to help you answer the questions.

Themes
Everyday situations, and a focus on sport, are used within the questions to put the maths into context.

NUMBER AND ALGEBRA

Negative numbers

Negative numbers are numbers below zero.
This arrow is pointing to negative 5 or minus 5.

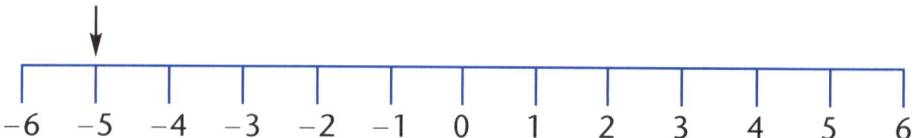

Bronze

a) What number is each arrow pointing to?

1. A   2. B   3. C   4. D

b) Put these negative numbers in order, smallest first:

1. −4 −7 −1 −5 −8
2. −12 −6 −15 −9 −21
3. −1 −8 −18 −12 −10

c) Look at this thermometer. Use it to answer these questions:

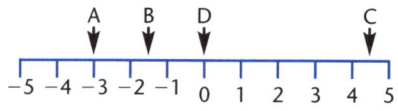

1. The thermometer says −3 degrees. It then rises by 8 degrees. What is the final reading?
2. The temperature falls from 7°C to −3°C. How many degrees does the temperature fall?
3. If the temperature in the evening is 5°C, how far must it fall to reach −2°C?

Silver

a) Put these numbers in order – lowest first:

1. −42, 6, 29, −45, −6
2. −35, −22, −56, −2, −44
3. 18, −9, −2, 12, −5
4. −22, −1, −19, −10, −9
5. 1, 0, −1, 2, −2

b) Jamie is recording his football team's weekly performance in the league. His team starts in 2nd place.

Week 1	Week 2	Week 3	Week 4	Week 5	Week 6
2nd place	−1	+2	0	−3	+1

1. What was his team's highest place?
2. Which week did this happen?
3. In which week did they make the biggest jump up?

Gold

a) Solve these problems:

1. −12 +  = 4
2. −5 + □ = 0
3. −5 + □ = −3
4. −4 + □ = 5
5. 14 − 19 =

b) In golf, the lower the score, the better. These are Tim's scores in 8 rounds of golf:

Round 1	−2	Round 5	−5
Round 2	3	Round 6	−3
Round 3	4	Round 7	1
Round 4	0	Round 8	−2

1. What was his lowest score?
2. What was his highest score?
3. What was his mean score?

Training Tips

• When counting up and down scales or number lines, don't forget to include the zero.

8

Square numbers

Square numbers

Square numbers are numbers that are the product of a number being multiplied by itself.

Example

36 is a square number because $6 \times 6 = 36$.

We say that 6^2 is 'six squared' so 6^2 is 36.

Bronze

a) Write these down in words.
   1. 2^2 2. 5^2 3. 7^2

b) Try these questions
   1. What is 5 squared?
   2. What is 9 squared?
   3. What is 8 squared?

c) Which of these are square numbers?
   1. 2 3 1 5 7
   2. 5 4 6 8 10
   3. 7 8 9 10 11
   4. 10 12 14 16 18

Silver

a) What is:
   1. 12^2 2. 15^2
   3. 17^2 4. 14^2

b) Use a calculator for these:
   1. What number, when multiplied by itself, gives 1225?
   2. Find two consecutive numbers with a product of 4160.
   3. The area of a square is 676 cm squared. What is the length of its sides?
   4. 7744 is what number squared?
   5. A square has an area of 1764 cm squared. What is the length of its sides?

Gold

a) What is:
   1. 33^2 2. 17^2
   3. 28^2 4. 99^2

b) Try these:
   1. What number, when multiplied by itself, gives 11 664?
   2. A square is 14 641 cm squared. What length are the sides?
   3. 12 769 is the product of what number squared?
   4. 101 squared is what?
   5. 41 616 is what squared?

Training Tips

- Learn all the square numbers up to 12×12 (1, 2, 4, 9, 16, 25, 36, 49, 64, 81, 100, 121, 144).

Factors and prime numbers

Factors

The pairs of factors for the number 18 are: 1 and 18, 2 and 9, 3 and 6

Prime numbers

A prime number is a number greater than 1 that only has two factors – itself and 1. The first 10 prime numbers are 2, 3, 5, 7, 11, 13, 17, 19, 23 and 29

What are the pairs of factors for these numbers?

1. 36
2. 44
3. 56
4. 24
5. 51
6. 99
7. 34
8. 64
9. 72
10. 80

Which of these are prime numbers?

1. 27, 29, 32, 33, 34
2. 30, 31, 32, 33, 34
3. 34, 35, 36, 37, 38
4. 85, 86, 87, 88, 89
5. 60, 61, 62, 63, 64
6. 40, 41, 42, 43, 44
7. 71, 72, 73, 74, 75
8. 96, 97, 98, 99, 100
9. 14, 25, 33, 43, 55
10. 55, 56, 57, 58, 59

Write down the next 20 Prime numbers after 100.

Training Tips

- Prime numbers are always odd, with the exception of the number 2.

NUMBER AND ALGEBRA

Fractions

Simplifying fractions

The fraction $\frac{4}{16}$ can be cancelled down to $\frac{1}{4}$ by dividing the numerator and the denominator by the same number – in this case 4.

Mixed numbers

The improper fraction $\frac{163}{10}$ is $16\frac{3}{10}$ when changed to a mixed number.

 **Bronze**

a) Complete these sentences:
1. Two sixths is the same as?
2. Two eights is the same as?
3. Four tenths is the same as?
4. Nine twelfths is the same as?
5. Twelve sixteenths is the same as?

b) Place these in order – smallest first:
1. $\frac{3}{5}, \frac{3}{6}, \frac{3}{8}, \frac{4}{9}, \frac{2}{5}$
2. $\frac{6}{9}, \frac{6}{10}, \frac{5}{8}, \frac{5}{9}, \frac{4}{5}$
3. $1\frac{3}{5}, 1\frac{5}{6}, 1\frac{5}{8}, 1\frac{6}{9}, 1\frac{3}{4}$
4. $\frac{3}{5}, \frac{4}{6}, \frac{7}{9}, \frac{9}{10}, \frac{8}{9}$
5. $1\frac{1}{2}, \frac{3}{4}, 1\frac{1}{4}, 2, \frac{1}{2}$

 **Silver**

a) Simplify these fractions to their lowest form:
1. $\frac{4}{12}$
2. $\frac{5}{25}$
3. $\frac{6}{12}$
4. $\frac{4}{16}$
5. $\frac{8}{12}$

b) Simplify these fractions and then order them smallest to biggest:
1. $2\frac{3}{10}, 1\frac{1}{2}, 2\frac{3}{4}, 2\frac{1}{10}$
2. $\frac{8}{12}, \frac{8}{16}, \frac{8}{10}, \frac{8}{9}$
3. $\frac{4}{6}, \frac{2}{5}, \frac{5}{10}, \frac{6}{9}$
4. $1\frac{2}{10}, 1\frac{2}{6}, 1\frac{4}{12}, 1\frac{6}{16}$
5. $3\frac{2}{6}, 2\frac{14}{16}, 3\frac{4}{8}, 4\frac{6}{9}$

 **Gold**

a) Simplify these fractions to their lowest form:
1. $\frac{36}{60}$
2. $\frac{49}{77}$
3. $\frac{55}{105}$
4. $\frac{56}{72}$
5. $\frac{9}{81}$

b) Convert these improper fractions to mixed numbers:
1. $\frac{145}{12}$
2. $\frac{54}{13}$
3. $\frac{123}{25}$
4. $\frac{118}{34}$
5. $\frac{189}{21}$

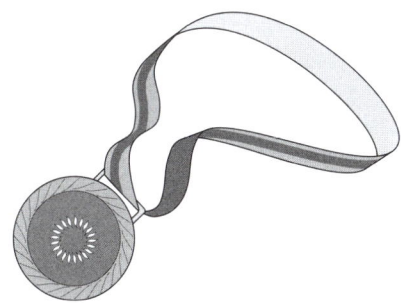

 **Training Tips**
- Learn as many fraction equivalents as you can. (e.g. $\frac{1}{3} = \frac{2}{6} = \frac{3}{9} = \frac{4}{12} = \frac{5}{15}$)

NUMBER AND ALGEBRA

Finding fractions of numbers and quantities

Finding a fifth of something is the same as dividing it by 5. For example to find a fifth of 15 we divide 15 by 5 to give the answer 3.

So, a $\frac{1}{5}$ of 15 is the same as 15 divided by 5.

Bronze

Find these fractions and amounts:

1. What is one tenth of 180?
2. What is $\frac{1}{4}$ of 80?
3. What is $\frac{3}{10}$ of 50?
4. What is $\frac{7}{10}$ of 250?
5. What is $\frac{4}{5}$ of 100?
6. What is $\frac{1}{10}$ of 1000?
7. What is $\frac{2}{3}$ of 99?
8. What is one quarter of 72?
9. What fraction of one week is 2 days?
10. What fraction of 1 l is 235 ml?

Silver

Find these fractions and amounts:

1. What is $\frac{7}{10}$ of 200?
2. What is $\frac{4}{5}$ of 45?
3. What is $\frac{5}{6}$ of 66?
4. What fraction of 1 metre is 65 cm?
5. What fraction of 1 kg is 483 g?
6. What fraction of one year is one week?
7. What is $\frac{3}{8}$ of 64?
8. What is $\frac{7}{9}$ of 81?
9. What is $\frac{24}{25}$ of 250?
10. What fraction of £5 is £1.25?

Gold

Find these fractions and amounts:

1. How many fifths in $24\frac{3}{5}$?
2. How many eighths in $41\frac{5}{8}$?
3. What is $\frac{7}{12}$ of 504?
4. Write $\frac{9}{100}$ of a km in millimetres.
5. What fraction of 10 litres is 5240 ml?
6. What fraction of a leap year is one weekend?
7. What is $\frac{1}{13}$ of 156?
8. What fraction of £20 is £2.25?
9. What fraction of 1 m is 25 mm?
10. What fraction of a week is 56 hours?

Training Tips

- To find $\frac{4}{5}$ of a number you could find one fifth and then multiply the answer by 4.

Fractions and decimals

Decimals are another way of writing fractions. For example, 0.05 is the same as $\frac{5}{100}$, 8.35 is the same as $8\frac{35}{100}$ and 9.341 m is the same as 9 m, 34 cm and 1 mm.

Fractions can be converted into decimals by dividing the numerator (top number) by the denominator (bottom number). You will need to use a calculator to do some of these.

 **Bronze**

a) Write these decimals as fractions.
1. 0.50
2. 0.75
3. 0.25

b) Write these fractions as decimals.
1. $\frac{25}{100}$
2. $\frac{7}{100}$
3. $\frac{77}{100}$

c) Convert these fractions to decimals. Round your answer to 2 decimal places.
1. $\frac{1}{2}$
2. $\frac{1}{4}$
3. $\frac{30}{100}$
4. $\frac{40}{100}$

 **Silver**

a) What are the decimal fraction equivalents of the following measurements?
1. 2 m, 32 cm and 6 mm
2. 10 m, 67 cm and 7 mm
3. 8 m, 32 cm and 9 mm

b) Write each of these decimals as a fraction.
1. 0.37
2. 4.1
3. 8.02

c) Convert these fractions to decimals. Round your answer to 2 decimal places.
1. $\frac{5}{10}$
2. $\frac{3}{4}$
3. $\frac{6}{8}$
4. $\frac{5}{8}$

 **Gold**

You can use a calculator for these if you want to.

a) Which of these is less?
1. $\frac{7}{9}$ or $\frac{4}{5}$?
2. $\frac{23}{25}$ or $\frac{7}{8}$?
3. 0.25 or $\frac{6}{25}$?

b) Place these in order – smallest first.
1. 0.45, $\frac{3}{5}$, 0.37, $\frac{4}{5}$
2. $\frac{12}{25}$, $\frac{5}{6}$, 0.70, 0.85
3. $\frac{13}{20}$, $\frac{17}{25}$, 0.69, 0.73

c) Convert these fractions to decimals. Round your answer to 2 decimal places.
1. $\frac{8}{40}$
2. $\frac{18}{20}$
3. $\frac{21}{25}$
4. $\frac{24}{27}$

 **Training Tips**

- When rounding, remember '5 or more round up, less than 5 round down'.
- Learn the decimal equivalents of these fractions:
  $\frac{1}{1000}$ = 0.001 $\frac{1}{8}$ = 0.125 $\frac{1}{3}$ = 0.333333̇ $\frac{2}{3}$ = 0.666666̇

NUMBER AND ALGEBRA

Fractions, decimals and percentages

Use these facts to help you answer the questions.

Fractions, decimals and percentages facts

One whole = 100% $1\% = 0.01 = \frac{1}{100}$
One half = 50% $10\% = 0.1 = \frac{1}{10}$
One quarter = 25% $20\% = 0.2 = \frac{1}{5}$
One tenth = 10% $25\% = 0.25 = \frac{1}{4}$
                     $50\% = 0.5 = \frac{1}{2}$
                     $57\% = 0.57 = \frac{57}{100}$
                     $75\% = 0.75 = \frac{3}{4}$

Using a calculator

You can find difficult percentages by using a calculator. Look at this question.

526 football fans were asked who their favourite player was. 290 said David Beckham. What percentage said David Beckham was their favourite player?

Use a calculator
Key in '290' then 'divide symbol' then '526' then '%'. You should have 55.133. Round this answer down to 55%.

Bronze

a) Try these questions without using a calculator:
1. What is 10% of 4 metres?
2. What is 75% of £100?
3. 25% of the people on the bus are wearing glasses. What percentage is not wearing glasses?
4. Dave got 30 out of 60 in his spelling test. Davina scored 35%. Who did better in the test – Dave or Davina?

b) Find these percentages by using halving and quartering.
1. 25% of £200
2. 50% of £260
3. 75% of £400
4. 25% of £280

Silver

a) What percentages are equivalent to these decimals?
1. 0.41   2. 0.78

b) Try these without using a calculator:
1. Find 60% of £60
2. Find 70% of 300kg
3. A pair of trainers cost £45. It has a 10% discount in a sale. What is the sale price of the trainers?

c) Find these percentages by halving and quartering:
1. 12.5% of £48 000
2. 6.25% of 12 m

Gold

Answer these questions using a calculator. Round the answers up or down.

a) Here are some Maths Test scores. What are their percentages?
1. Ben – 139 out of 146
2. Tanya – 141 out of 146
3. Andrea – 125 out of 146

b) How many out of 146 did each of these children score?
1. Leo – 85%
2. Finley – 92%
3. Jamie – 89%
4. Bruce – 67%
5. Alexa – 99%

Training Tips

• To find 1% of something, first find 10% then find 10% of THAT answer. You can work out any percentage by adding all the 10%, 5% and 1% answers together!

14

NUMBER AND ALGEBRA

Multiplication – grid and partitioning methods

Using a grid shows clearly which numbers are being multiplied. Always approximate first so you will know if your answer is sensible.

82 × 38 is approximately 80 × 40 = 3200

×	30	8		
80	2400	640	=	3040
2	60	16	=	76
			=	3116

The partitioning method is the most common method of multiplying – you should be familiar with it already.

Check against the approximation.

Short multiplication

246 × 9 =

Approximate first.
250 × 10 = 2500

```
   246
 ×   9
  2214
    45
```

Long multiplication

72 × 48 =

Approximate first.
70 × 50 = 3500

```
    72
 ×  48
  2880   (72 × 40)
   576   (72 × 8)
  3456   (add the two together)
    11
```

a) Try these:
1. 38 × 49   2. 94 × 83
3. 66 × 44   4. 29 × 79

b) Try these short and long multiplications using partitioning.
1. 923 × 4   2. 835 × 7
3. 612 × 8   4. 929 × 9
5. 72 × 43   6. 84 × 52
7. 91 × 79   8. 48 × 67

a) Try these:
1. 735 × 36   2. 601 × 48
3. 377 × 27   4. 193 × 13

b) Try these short and long multiplications:
1. 9334 × 7   2. 6317 × 6
3. 4431 × 8   4. 429 × 62
5. 882 × 37   6. 749 × 55

a) Use the grid method to solve these calculations. Remember to approximate first.
1. 8352 × 38   2. 4427 × 59
3. 7618 × 35   4. 2094 × 89

b) Have a go at multiplying these decimals:
1. 7.45 × 38   2. 6.24 × 52
3. 3.18 × 65   4. 9.67 × 43
5. 8.84 × 72   6. 4.31 × 26
7. 5.03 × 97   8. 1.67 × 88

Training Tips
- Check your final answer against your approximation – if they are not close, check them both.
- Remember to keep the place value when you multiply by tens, hundreds or thousands.

NUMBER AND ALGEBRA

Division – using multiples of the divider

Look carefully at this division calculation.
It can be completed using knowledge of the multiples of the divider.

Method 1   268 ÷ 8

268 − 80 = 188 (10 × 8)
188 − 80 = 108 (10 × 8)
108 − 80 = 28 (10 × 8)
28 − 24 = 4 (3 × 8)

33 lots of 8 have been taken away so our answer is 33 remainder 4.

Method 2   974 ÷ 32

Approximate first. 1000 ÷ 30 = 33

974 − 320 = 654 (10 × 32)
654 − 320 = 334 (10 × 32)
334 − 320 = 14 (10 × 32)

Answer: $30\frac{14}{32}$

Answer these using Method 1. Remember to approximate first and set your working out as clearly as you can.

1. 625 ÷ 6
2. 834 ÷ 9
3. 701 ÷ 5
4. 246 ÷ 4
5. 137 ÷ 7
6. 368 ÷ 2
7. 567 ÷ 3
8. 986 ÷ 8
9. 477 ÷ 7
10. 385 ÷ 5

Use Method 1 or 2 to answer these:

1. 738 ÷ 24
2. 695 ÷ 27
3. 374 ÷ 19
4. 981 ÷ 67
5. 583 ÷ 43
6. 461 ÷ 55
7. 264 ÷ 39
8. 197 ÷ 34
9. 806 ÷ 63
10. 537 ÷ 21

Use Method 1 or 2 to answer these:

1. 4825 ÷ 28
2. 7724 ÷ 62
3. 6018 ÷ 37
4. 1734 ÷ 44
5. 2956 ÷ 37
6. 3271 ÷ 53
7. 9816 ÷ 91
8. 5387 ÷ 72
9. 6731 ÷ 19
10. 2371 ÷ 82

Training Tips

- Be clear in your writing – it can show how you're thinking.

Division – short and long division

Short division is dividing by a single digit number.

Example   194 ÷ 6

Approximate first. 200 ÷ 5 = 40

```
      34 r 2
  6)194
   − 180
      14
   −  12
       2
```

Answer 34 r 2

Long division is dividing by a number with more than one digit.

Example   964 ÷ 38

Approximate first. 1000 ÷ 40 = 25

```
       25 r 14
  38)964
    − 760
      204
    − 190
       14
```

Answer 25 r 14

Bronze

Answer these short division calculations. Give remainders where appropriate.

1. 762 ÷ 3
2. 589 ÷ 6
3. 938 ÷ 5
4. 671 ÷ 8
5. 208 ÷ 2
6. 367 ÷ 7
7. 481 ÷ 9
8. 846 ÷ 4
9. 773 ÷ 6
10. 137 ÷ 9

Silver

Work out these long division sums:

1. 582 ÷ 25
2. 896 ÷ 62
3. 723 ÷ 34
4. 907 ÷ 71
5. 648 ÷ 24
6. 840 ÷ 35
7. 367 ÷ 41
8. 284 ÷ 19
9. 961 ÷ 93
10. 633 ÷ 72

Gold

Work out these long division sums:

1. 5872 ÷ 34
2. 4723 ÷ 56
3. 6791 ÷ 99
4. 7824 ÷ 22
5. 3015 ÷ 67
6. 2491 ÷ 82
7. 8632 ÷ 74
8. 1157 ÷ 13
9. 9257 ÷ 31
10. 4238 ÷ 64

Training Tips

- You can divide decimal numbers by whole numbers using these methods.

NUMBER AND ALGEBRA

Understanding multiplication and division

Look at this question: 4 + 7 × 5 = 39

Is the answer correct? The answer would be 55 if we add 4 and 7 and then multiply the answer by 5.

We can use brackets...
Now look at the calculation again.

4 + (7 × 5) = 39
4 + 35 = 39

Division is related to fractions.

$\frac{1}{4}$ of 24 is the same as 24 ÷ 4.

5 divided by 7 is the same as $\frac{5}{7}$.

17 divided by 9 is the same as 1 and $\frac{8}{9}$.

Bronze

a) Use brackets to make these correct:
  1. 6 + 8 × 9 = 78
  2. 7 − 3 × 4 = 16
  3. 2 × 6 + 7 = 19
  4. 8 × 3 + 7 = 80
  5. 9 − 7 × 3 = 6

b) Work these out:
  1. Share 56 by 7
  2. Divide 36 by 12
  3. What is the remainder when 84 is divided by 7?
  4. What are the factors of 24?
  5. How many groups of 9 can be made from 83?

Silver

a) Work these out:
  1. 0.4 × 7 = ☐
  2. 25 × ☐ = 8000
  3. 123 × 45 = ☐
  4. ☐ × 67 = 1541

b) Work these out:
  1. What are the factors of 84?
  2. What is the remainder when you divide 853 by 29?
  3. Divide 632 by 19.
  4. Share 455 by 35.

c) Complete these:
  1. $\frac{1}{5}$ of 30 is the same as ☐ or ☐
  2. 2.8 divided by 0.7 is the same as ☐

Gold

Work these out:
  1. (63 + 22) × 705 = ☐
  2. 124 × (92 − 29) = ☐
  3. (54 + 12) × 305 = ☐
  4. 428 × (39 + 17) = ☐
  5. (99 − 37) × 143 = ☐
  6. (476 + 382) ÷ (566 − 352)
  7. (222 + 429) ÷ 81
  8. 1569 ÷ (234 − 108)
  9. 7296 divided by 193
  10. (923 − 101) ÷ (1502 − 1487)
  11. 4502 divided by 793
  12. (250 ÷ 10) + (529 ÷ 23)

Training Tips

- It doesn't matter which way round you multiply numbers – the answer is the same.
- Division is not 'commutative'. This means that 21 ÷ 7 is not the same as 7 ÷ 21.

NUMBER AND ALGEBRA

Using a calculator

If a question has brackets in it you must **work out the brackets first** using your calculator. Write this answer down and then finish working out the sum.

> What is £10.99 less 25%?
> We type 10.99 − 25 % = 8.2425
> Round the answer: £8.24

 **Bronze**

a) Use your calculator to solve these two step problems:

1. 4 × (34 − 13) =
2. (190 − 84) × 2 =
3. 500 − (23 × 8) =
4. 325 − (12 × 12) =
5. (130 × 11) − 1200 =

b) Solve these measures problems using your calculator:

1. £4.56 − £1.27 =
2. 235 m × 4 =
3. 1.67 l − 0.58 l =
4. 3.34 kg × 8 =
5. £127.34 − £108.39 =

 **Silver**

a) Use your calculator to solve these multi-step problems:

1. (32 + 24) × (18 − 4) =
2. (123 − 116) × (908 − 889) =
3. (23 × 5) − 720 =

b) Solve these measures problems using your calculator:

1. £2.56 − ☐ = £1.29
2. 23.56 kg ÷ 4 =
3. 679 ml + 435 ml =

c) Solve these percentage problems using your calculator:

1. £3.56 less 25%
2. £12.99 plus 15%
3. £18.99 less 20%

Gold

a) Use your calculator to solve these multi-step problems:

1. (92 + 54) ÷ (193 − 187) =
2. (467 − 328) × (105 − 79) =
3. (86 × 13) − 1068 =

b) Solve these measures problems using your calculator:

1. £862.94 − ☐ = £352.78
2. 194.5 kg ÷ 7 =
3. 1.893 l + 435 ml =

c) Solve these percentage problems using your calculator:

1. £9.34 less 23%
2. £9.99 plus 17%
3. £168.97 less 29%

 **Training Tips**
- Remember that calculators don't put in all the decimals, so £3.20 will look like 3.2.

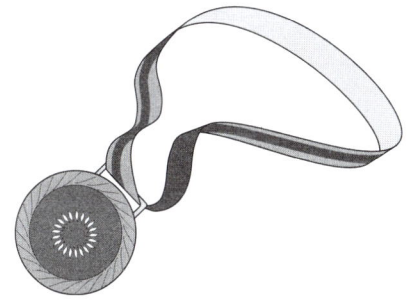

NUMBER AND ALGEBRA

Checking results of calculations

It is important that we check our answers to make sure they make sense and that we have not made a mistake. Over the next two pages you will practise this skill.

The inverse operation using a calculator

When you are using a calculator to work out sums, check you have got the right answer by putting in the inverse operation.

> If you have worked out 345 × 32 = 11 040
>
> check this is correct by typing in 11 040 ÷ 32 = 345
> You were correct.

Divisibility tests

You can check whether your division sums are correct by using these 'divisibility tests'.

By 3

A number is divisible by 3 if when you add up the digits in the number the answer divides by 3 with no remainders.

> *Example*
>
> 345 621 = 3 + 4 + 5 + 6 + 2 + 1 = 21
>
> Yes, 21 divides perfectly by 3, seven times, so 345 621 must be divisible by three.

By 2, 4 and 8

A number is divisible by 2 if the last digit is divisible by 2.

A number is divisible by 4 if the last two digits are divisible by 4.

A number is divisible by 8 if the last three digits are divisible by 8.

> *Example*
>
> 234 532 – is divisible by 2 ($\frac{2}{2}$) and 4 ($\frac{32}{4}$) but not 8 ($\frac{532}{8}$)

By 5 and 10

If a number ends in 5 or 0 then it is divisible by 5.

If a number ends in a 0 then it is divisible by 10

By 6 and 9

If a number is divisible by 2 AND 3 then it is divisible by 6.

> *Example*
>
> 928 566 is divisible by 2 (464 283) and 3 (309 522) so it must be divisible by 6.
>
> If the sum of the digits is divisible exactly by 9 then the number is divisible by 9.
>
> 6489 = 6 + 4 + 8 + 9 = 27 … which is divisible by 9!

NUMBER AND ALGEBRA

Bronze

a) Check the following sums using your calculator. Mark them right or wrong.
1. 289 × 13 = 3767
2. 43 488 ÷ 3624 = 12
3. 671 − 41 = 626
4. 164 × 127 = 21 828
5. 7176 ÷ 79 = 92

b) Check whether these sums are divisible exactly. Then complete the sums.
1. 918 ÷ 9 =
2. 3265 ÷ 10 =
3. 34 568 ÷ 4 =
4. 42171 ÷ 3 =
5. 127 979 ÷ 5 =
6. 9208 ÷ 2 =
7. 1217 ÷ 4 =
8. 966 ÷ 6 =
9. 12 664 ÷ 8 =
10. 255 550 ÷ 10 =

Silver

a) Check the following sums using your calculator. Mark them right or wrong.
1. 1789 × 16 = 28 624
2. 2584 ÷ 152 = 18
3. 7293 − 512 = 6783
4. 137 × 98 = 13 426
5. 7245 ÷ 70 = 105

b) Check whether these sums are divisible exactly. Then complete the sums.
1. 632 701 ÷ 9 =
2. 19 224 ÷ 8 =
3. 98 016 ÷ 4 =
4. 62 001 ÷ 3 =
5. 1 290 554 ÷ 5 =
6. 1048 ÷ 2 =
7. 71 507 ÷ 4 =
8. 468 ÷ 6 =
9. 10 783 ÷ 8 =
10. 196 325 ÷ 10 =

Gold

a) Check the following sums using your calculator. Mark them right or wrong.
1. 92 × 45 = 4410
2. 11 772 ÷ 108 = 109
3. 3268 − 1783 = 1458
4. 176 × 143 = 25 168
5. 6745 ÷ 71 = 95

b) Check whether these sums are divisible exactly. Then complete the sums.
1. 1 634 301 ÷ 9 =
2. 18 327 ÷ 8 =
3. 108 443 ÷ 4 =
4. 73 023 ÷ 3 =
5. 22 345 ÷ 5 =
6. 2227 ÷ 2 =
7. 109 752 ÷ 4 =
8. 978 ÷ 6 =
9. 93 136 ÷ 8 =
10. 2 876 320 ÷ 10 =

Training Tips

- Checking every sum will make sure you won't make mistakes.
- Checking sums:
  Change the order to check.
  Do an equivalent sum.

SHAPE, SPACE AND MEASURES

Length, mass and capacity – reading scales 1

Once you have chosen which measuring instrument to use to measure something, it's important that you can read it accurately!

a) Look carefully at these different rulers. What is the difference between the arrows in centimetres?

1.

2.
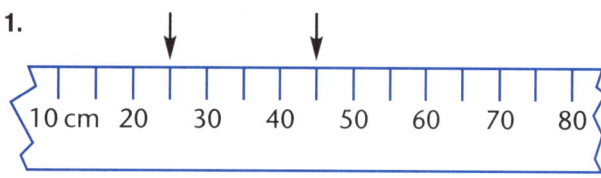

3.
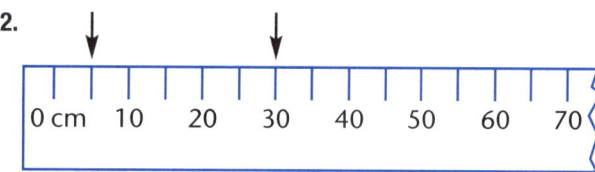

b) Add 80 ml to each cylinder. What is the new water level?

1.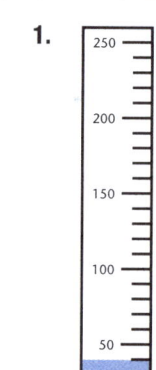
2.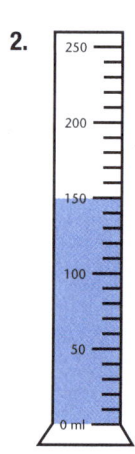
3.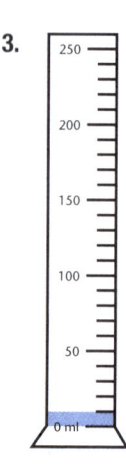

c) Take 400 grams from each set of scales. How much is left?

1.
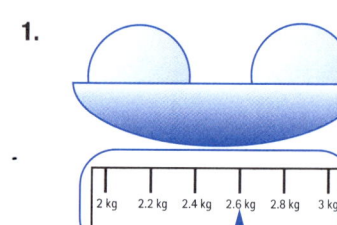

2.
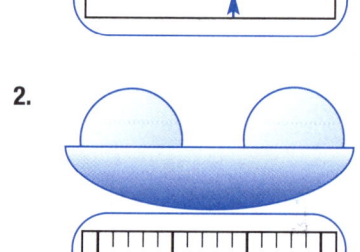

Training Tips

- Always check the units of measurement on any measuring instrument. If the instrument is showing '0.25', then 0.25 what? Centimetres? Metres?

SHAPE, SPACE AND MEASURES

Silver

a) Look at these rulers. What distance is the arrow pointing to in centimetres?

1.
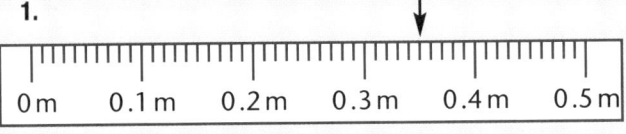

2.
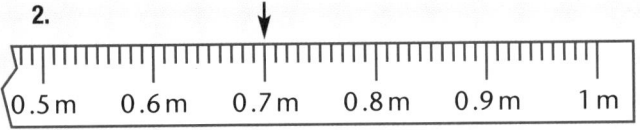

3.
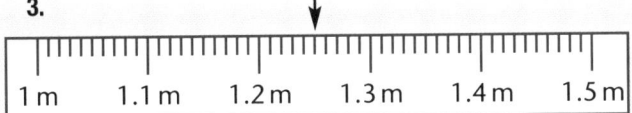

b) How many grams are on each of these scales?

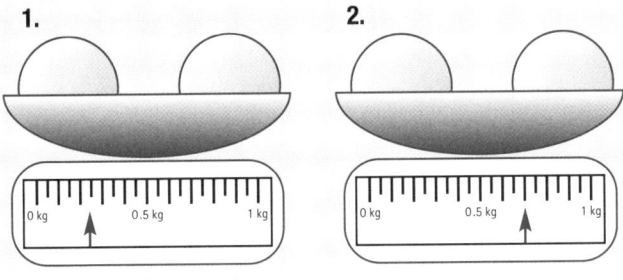

c) How many millilitres of water are in each of these cylinders?

1.
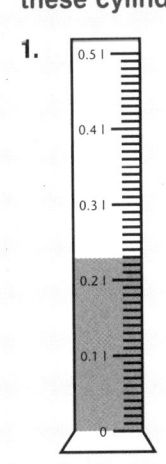

2.
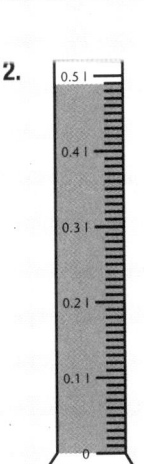

Gold

a) Look at these rulers. What distance is the arrow pointing to in centimetres?

1.
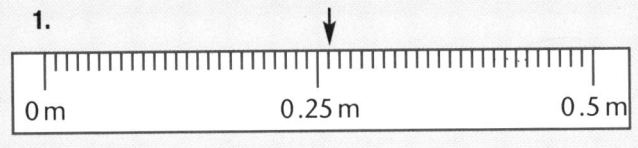

2.
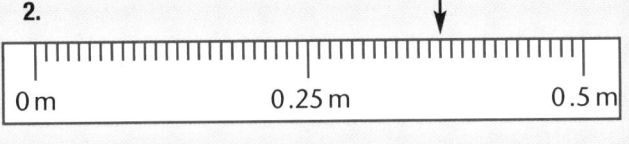

3.
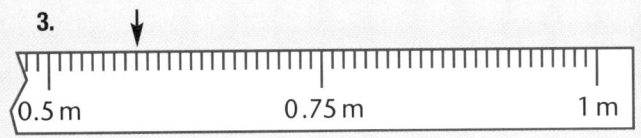

b) How many grams are on each of these scales?

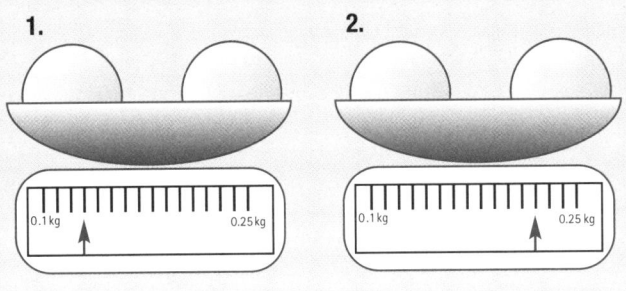

c) What do you think each of these instruments measures?

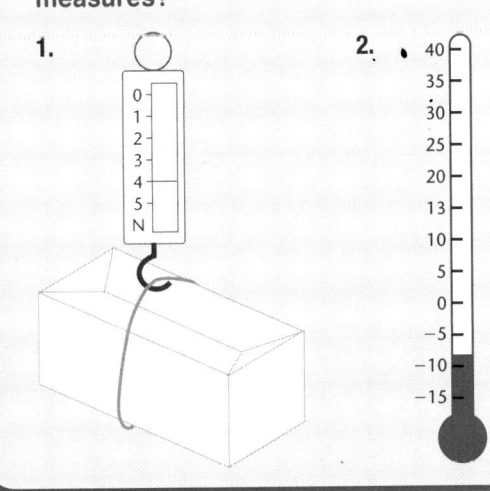

SHAPE, SPACE AND MEASURES

Length, mass and capacity – reading scales 2

Remember the key facts about measuring:

10 mm = 1 cm	1000 g = 1 kg	1000 ml = 1 l
100 cm = 1 m		
1000 m = 1 km		

Bronze

a) Convert these measures into kilograms, litres, metres or kilometres:

1. 1500 g 2. 250 ml 3. 600 cm
4. 3250 g 5. 500 ml 6. 750 m

b) Round these measurements to the nearest whole unit:

1. 50.3 m 2. 4.7 l 3. 1.95 m

c) Round these measurements to the nearest kilogram, litre or metre:

1. 3576 ml 2. 721 cm 3. 1019 g
4. 8753 ml 5. 10 567 cm

Silver

a) Convert these measures into kilograms, litres, metres or kilometres:

1. 2230 g 2. 110 ml
3. 730 cm 4. 1950 g
5. 320 ml 6. 1390 m

b) Use the scale opposite to approximate the following:

1. The number of litres in 3.5 gallons.
2. The number of gallons in 5 litres.
3. How many gallons there are in 12 litres.

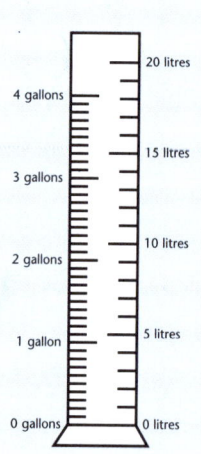

c) Use this centimetres and inches ruler to approximate the following:

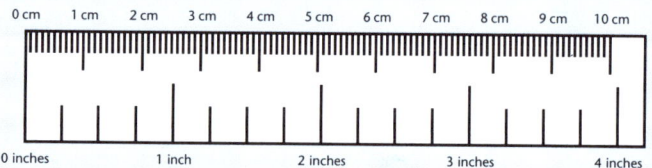

1. The number of mm in $\frac{1}{2}$ an inch.
2. The number of inches in 7.5 cm.
3. How many cm in 2 inches?
4. How many cm in 3 inches?
5. How many inches in 90 mm?

SHAPE, SPACE AND MEASURES

Gold

a) Convert these measures into kilograms, litres, metres or kilometres:

1. 1062 g
2. 428 ml
3. 139 cm
4. 364 g
5. 18 ml
6. 7116 m

b) Use the scale opposite to approximate the following:

1. 0.5 gallons in ml
2. 4 l in gallons
3. 0.75 gallons in l

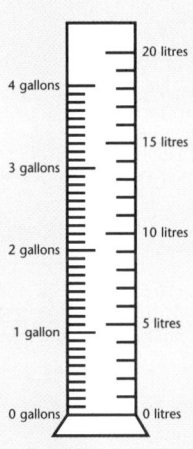

c) Use this centimetres and inches ruler to calculate the following:

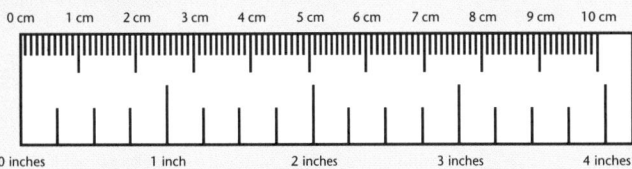

1. The number of mm in $\frac{1}{4}$ of an inch.
2. The number of inches in 5.1 cm.
3. Estimate how many cm there are in 6 inches?
4. Estimate how many inches there are in 1 m?
5. How many mm in 1 inch?

Training Tips
- Read scales carefully. Make sure you know what units you are writing down.

SHAPE, SPACE AND MEASURES

Perimeter

Perimeter is the distance around a 2D shape.

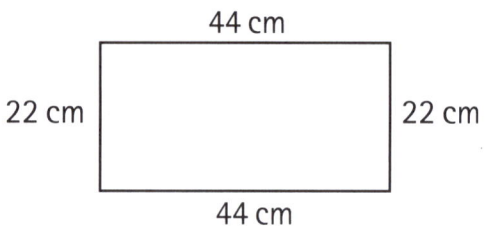

Example
Perimeter = 44 cm + 22 cm + 44 cm + 22 cm
= 132 cm

Bronze

Answer these questions:

1. A rectangle has a shortest side of 8 cm and a longest side of 12 cm. What is the perimeter?

2. The perimeter of a rectangle is 45 cm. The length of the longest side is 16 cm. What is the length of the shortest side?

3. The perimeter of a rectangle is 68 cm. The shortest side is 10 cm. What is the length of the longest side?

4. The perimeter of a rectangle is 82 m. The shortest side is 12 m. What is the length of the longest side?

5. The perimeter of a rectangle is 12 cm. The length of the longest side is 4 cm. What is the length of the shortest side?

6. A rectangle has a shortest side of 13 m and a longest side of 24 m. What is the perimeter?

7. The perimeter of a rectangle is 102 cm. The shortest side is 18 cm. What is the length of the longest side?

8. The perimeter of a rectangle is 161 cm. The length of the longest side is 65 cm. What is the length of the shortest side?

Training Tips

- The formula for finding the perimeter of a rectangle is 'two times the length and breadth' or $2 \times (l + b)$.

SHAPE, SPACE AND MEASURES

Silver

Draw these shapes and write in the lengths you know. Work out the missing lengths (in units). Now find the perimeter.

1.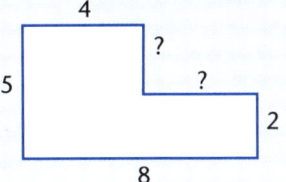

2.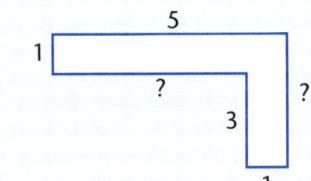

3.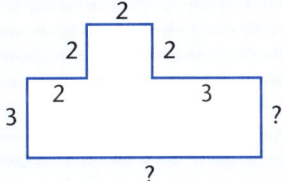

4.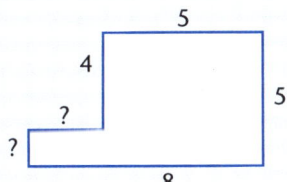

5.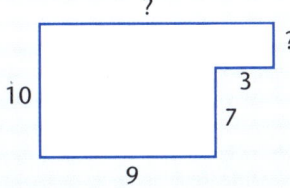

Gold

Draw these shapes and write in the lengths you know. Work out the missing lengths (in units). Now find the perimeter.

1.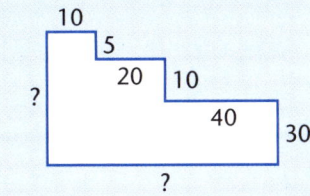

2.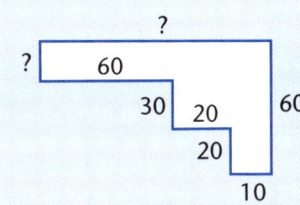

3.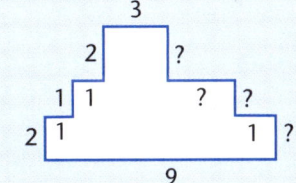

4.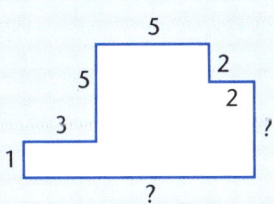

5.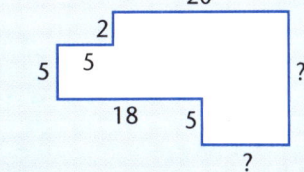

27

SHAPE, SPACE AND MEASURES

Area

Area is the space that is covered by a shape.

You can find the area of a right-angled triangle by turning it into a rectangle, finding the area of the rectangle and then halving your answer.

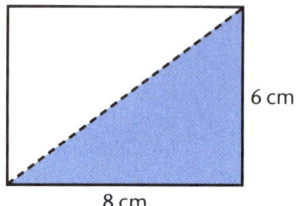

Area of this right-angled triangle = 24 cm^2

a) What is the approximate area of these rectangles? Remember that these are scale drawings. Don't try to measure them – use the formula.

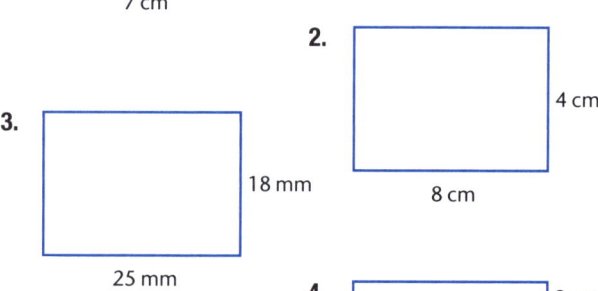

b) Use your knowledge of area to answer these questions:

1. Would you expect the area of the classroom floor to be 4 m^2, 40 m^2 or 400 m^2?

2. Would you expect the area of a postcard to be 8 cm^2, 80 cm^2 or 800 cm^2?

3. Is the area of a football pitch about 5 m^2, 500 m^2 or 5000 m^2?

4. Is the area of this book about 100 cm^2, 10 cm^2 or 600 cm^2?

5. Which of these is more likely to be the area of a postage stamp? 150 mm^2, 1500 mm^2 or 10 mm^2.

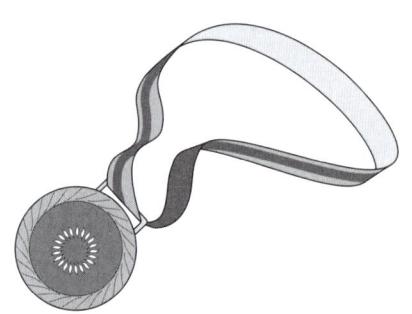

- Always use mm^2 or cm^2 or m^2 when writing your area answers.

Training Tips

28

SHAPE, SPACE AND MEASURES

a) Find the area of these shapes. Split them into rectangles to help you.

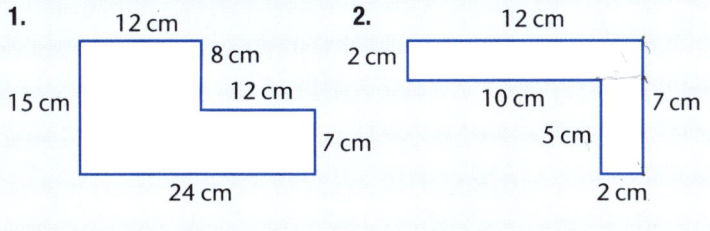

b) Use the information in the introduction to work out the area of these triangles:

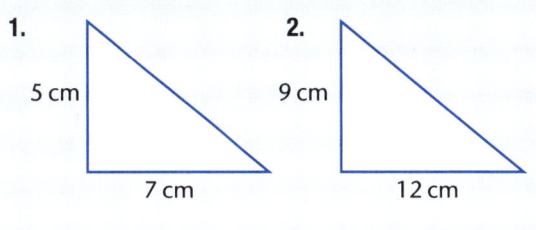

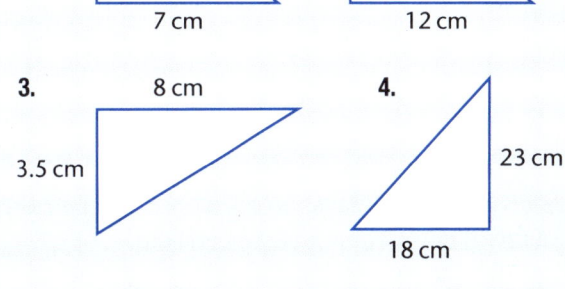

a) Find the area of these shapes:

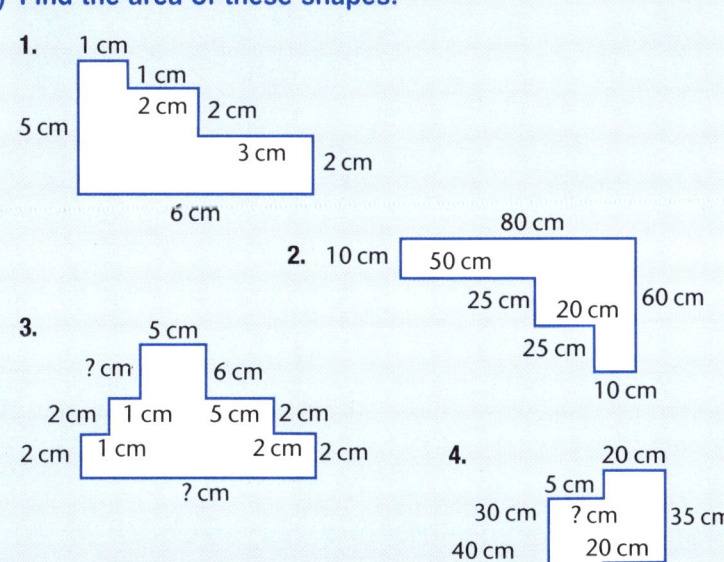

b) Without using a calculator, find the total surface area of these cuboids. Remember each has 6 faces!

1.
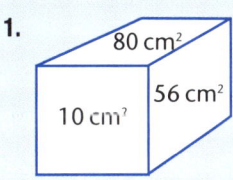

2.
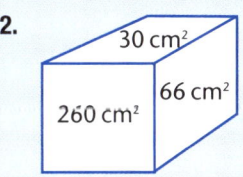

3.
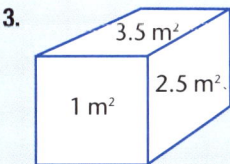

4.
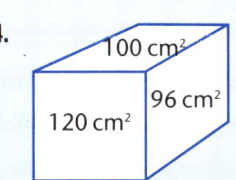

29

SHAPE, SPACE AND MEASURES

Time

Greenwich Mean Time (GMT) is the time measured from the Greenwich Royal Observatory in London. All other times in the world are either ahead of or behind GMT.

Hawaii	2:00	−10
Los Angeles	4:00	−8
Chicago	6:00	−6
New York	7:00	−5
GMT	**12:00 Midday**	**0**
Rome	13:00	+1
Istanbul	14:00	+2
Kuwait	15:00	+3
Delhi	17:00	+5
Bangkok	19:00	+7
Beijing	20:00	+8
Tokyo	21:00	+9
Canberra	22:00	+10
Wellington	0:00	+12

Bronze

a) At 13:00 in London, what time is it in these cities?
1. Kuwait
2. Tokyo
3. New York
4. Los Angeles
5. Bangkok

b) Use the world chart to answer these questions:
1. When the time is 14:30 in London, what time is it in Istanbul?
2. When children are having breakfast in London, what are children probably doing in Delhi?

3. When school finishes at 16:00 in Rome, are children in Bangkok at school?
4. If I wake up in New York at 8.00 a.m., what time is it in Istanbul?
5. When children go to bed at 21:00 in Chicago, what time is it in London?

SHAPE, SPACE AND MEASURES

a) Use the world time chart to answer these questions:

1. When the time is 4:10 in London, what meal are people in Bejing eating?
2. When the time is 12:00 in Los Angeles, would any children be at school in England?
3. When school finishes at 15:30 in Istanbul, are schools likely to be open in Delhi?
4. If the time is midday in Canberra, what time is it in Hawaii?
5. If it is 7:22 in Wellington, what time is it in New York?

b) If it is midday in these places, what time is it in London?

1. Kuwait
2. Bangkok
3. Canberra
4. Chicago
5. Delhi

The Medal Maths airline flies to each of these destinations about four times a day.
Copy and complete the timetable. Remember all times are local. The first row has been done for you.

London	Istanbul (+2hrs)	Delhi (+5hrs)	Beijing (+8hrs)	Canberra (+10hrs)	Los Angeles (–8hrs)	New York (–5hrs)
Flight time	5hrs	7.5hrs	12hrs	24hrs	12hrs	7hrs
08:00	15:00	20:30	04:00	18:00 (the next day!)	12:00	10:00
12:30					16:30	
16:00				02:00		
20:30		09:00				
21:45	04:45					
23:15						01:15

Training Tips

- If your times go over the 24 hours then do the calculation in stages.

31

SHAPE, SPACE AND MEASURES

2D shapes

2D Shapes have corners and sides. They can also have parallel lines, equal sides, lines of symmetry and equal angles. Look at these examples.

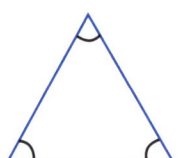 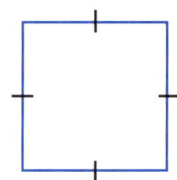 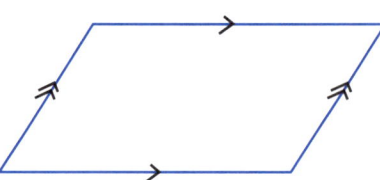 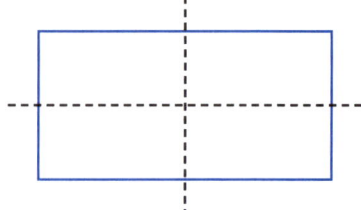

a) Write the name of each of these shapes:

1. 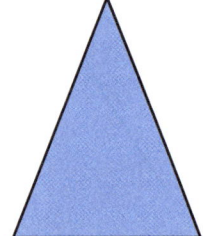 2. 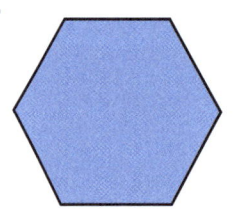 3.  4.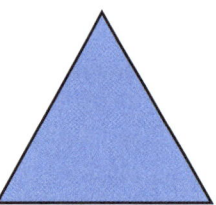

5. 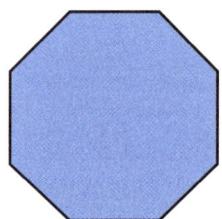 6. 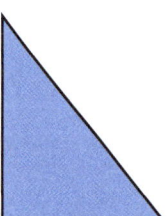 7. 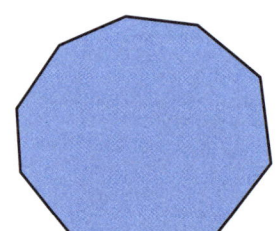 8.

b) Write three properties of a rectangle.

c) Write two properties of an equilateral triangle.

d) Write three properties of a square.

- Keep a note of the properties of different shapes. Include how many sides and whether each has parallel lines, equal sides or lines of symmetry.

SHAPE, SPACE AND MEASURES

a) Name these shapes:

1.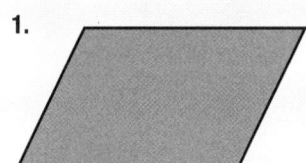
2.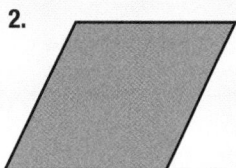
3.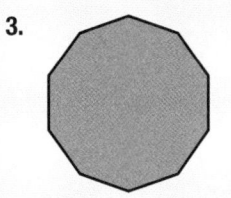
4.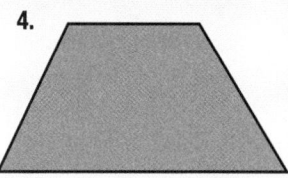
5.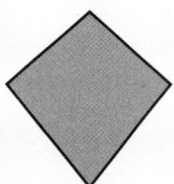
6.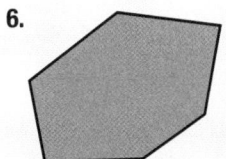
7.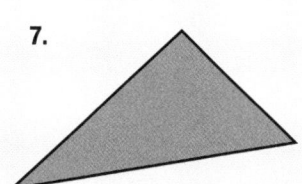
8.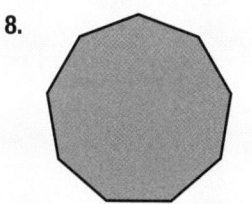

b) Write a description of each of the shapes above next to its name. Remember to include the different properties.

a) Draw these shapes:

1. Parallelogram
2. Rhombus
3. Square
4. Rectangle
5. Kite
6. Equilateral triangle
7. Scalene triangle
8. Right-angled triangle

b) Copy and complete this table by adding the names of the shapes above. Some may appear in more than one column.

Opposite sides that are parallel	2 equal sides	4 equal sides	2 equal angles	3 or more equal angles	Adjacent sides are equal	Diagonals bisect

33

SHAPE, SPACE AND MEASURES

Properties of 3D shapes

3D shapes are solid shapes.

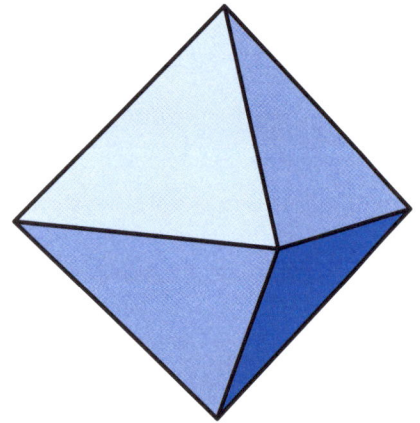

This is an 'octahedron'.

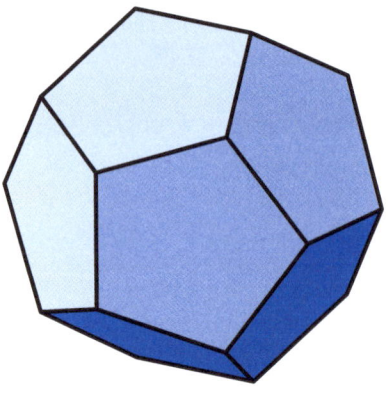

This is a 'dodecahedron'.

Copy these shapes and name them:

1.

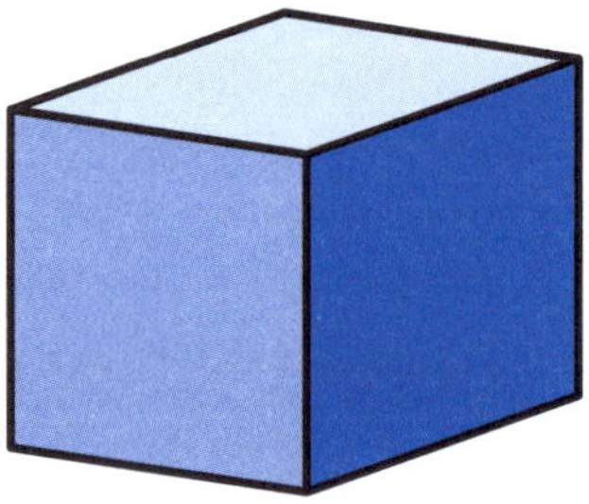

2.

3.

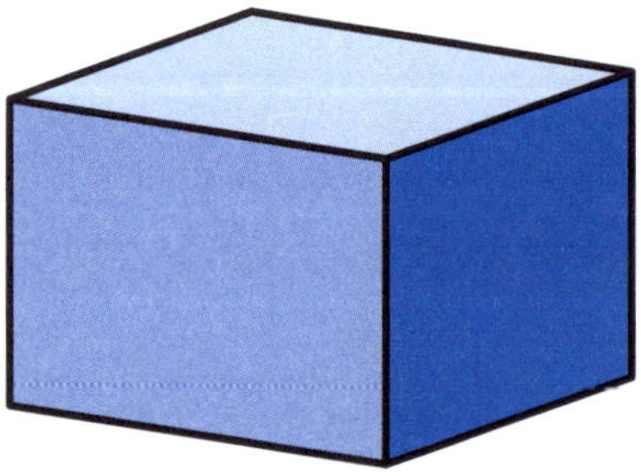

4.

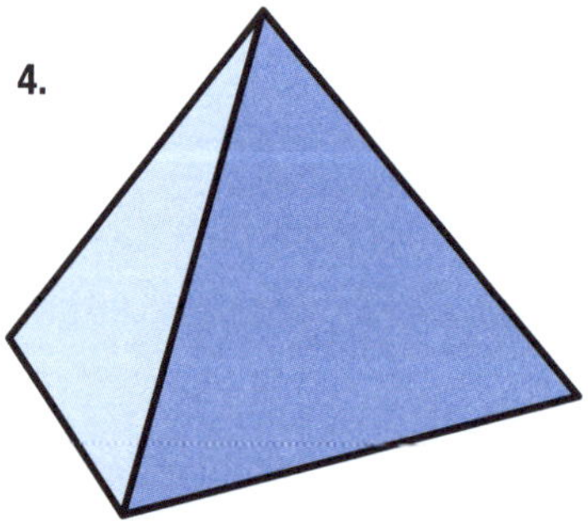

● Keep a note of any names of shapes along with a sketch drawing. This will help you to remember them.

Training Tips

34

SHAPE, SPACE AND MEASURES

Silver

Copy each of these shapes and name them.
Next to the shape write the number of faces and edges.
Draw another shape with one more face than each of these.

1. 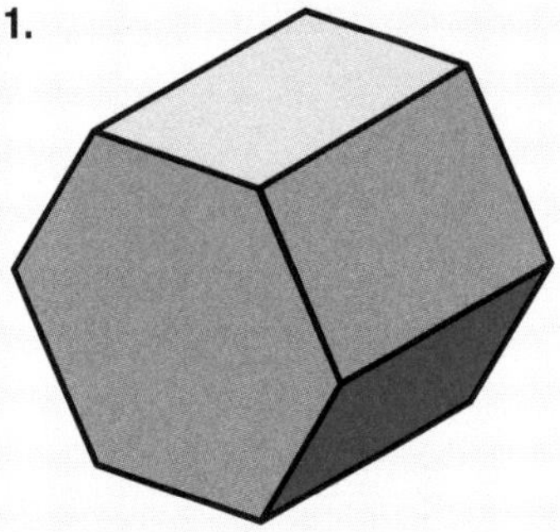
2. 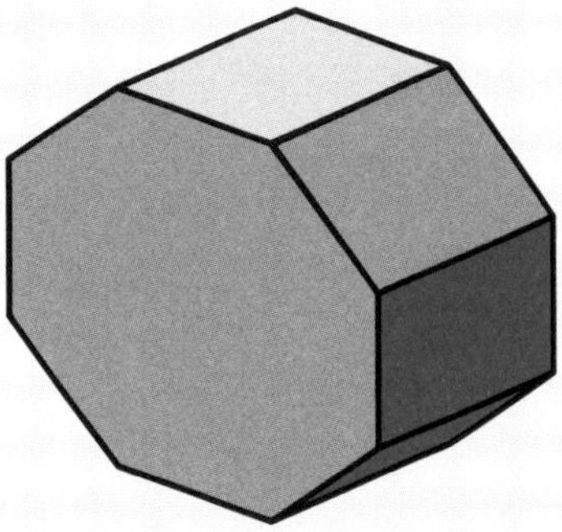
3. 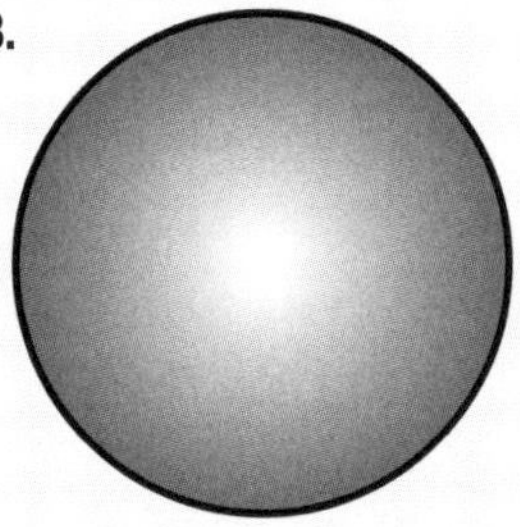
4.

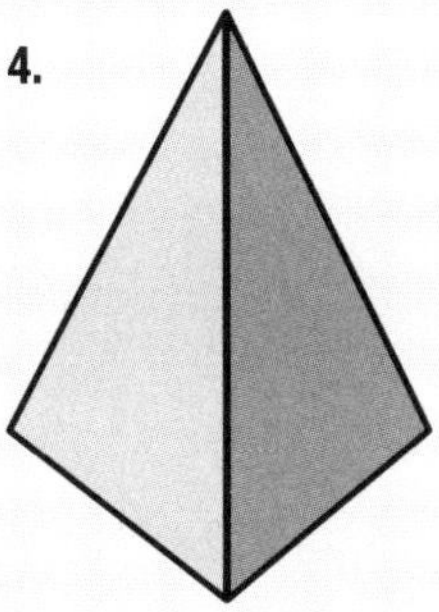

Gold

Copy each of these shapes and name them.
Next to the name write whether the shape has parallel faces or edges.

1. 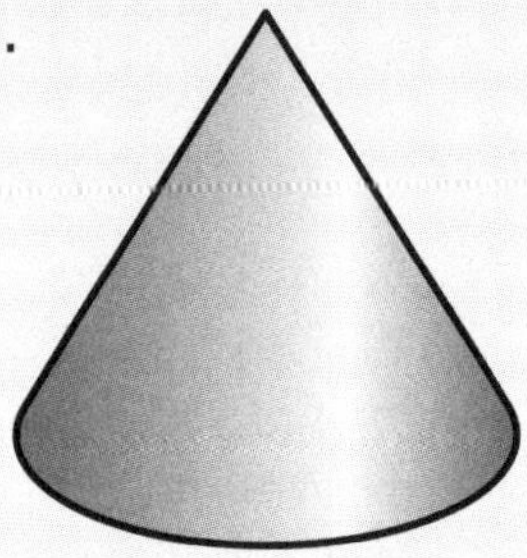
2. 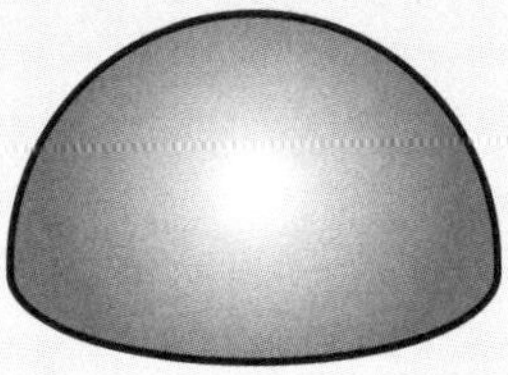
3. 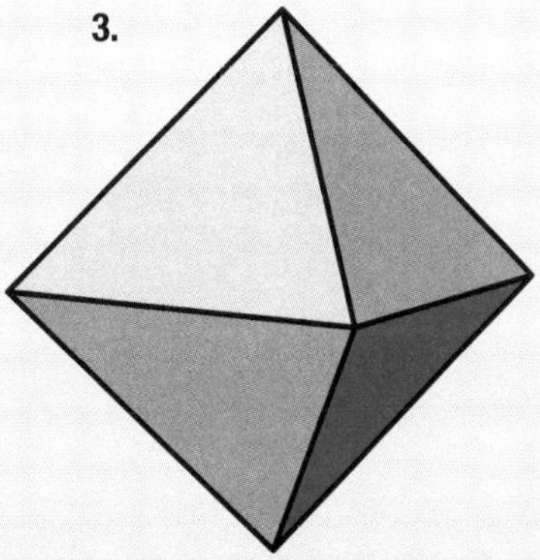
4.

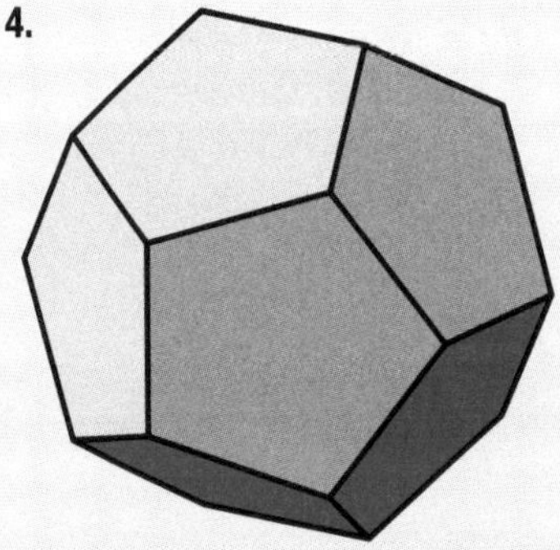

SHAPE, SPACE AND MEASURES

Position and direction

Key Facts

Perpendicular lines are at right angles to each other.

Parallel lines are the same distance apart – they never meet.

Two lines that cross each other are called intersecting lines. The point at which they cross is called an intersection.

A diagonal is a straight line that joins the vertices of a polygon.

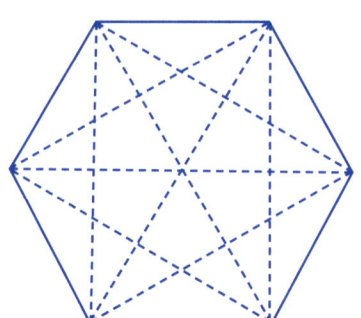

Bronze

a) Draw x and y axes on squared paper.
   Now copy these shapes and answer the questions.

   1. These points are the coordinates of the vertices of a shape: (2, 3) (2, 7) (4, 3) (4, 7). What is the name of the shape?

   2. Three of the vertices of a square are (4, 1), (4, 3) and (6, 3). What are the coordinates of the 4th vertex?

   3. Plot these coordinates: (4, 2) (6, 2) (4, 5) (6, 5). What is the name of the shape?

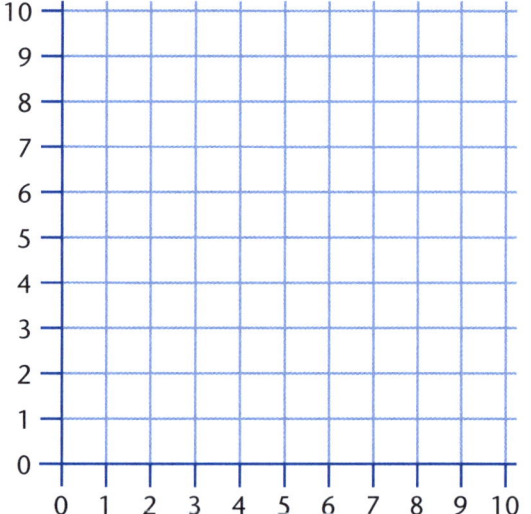

b) Draw these shapes. Circle the perpendicular lines in blue. Circle the parallel lines in red and draw in the diagonal lines (a straight line from a vertex to a non–adjacent vertex).

   1.   2.   3.

SHAPE, SPACE AND MEASURES

Silver

You will need to plot points in all four quadrants to answer these. Draw this on squared paper.

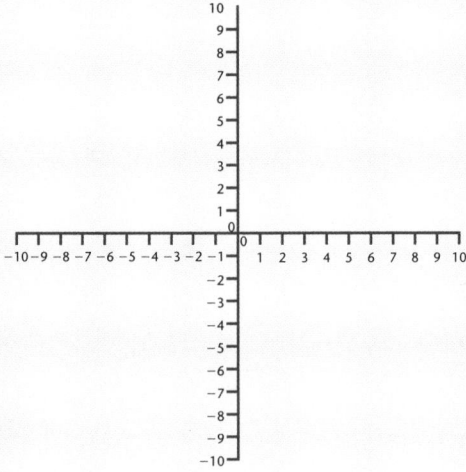

1. Three of the vertices of a rectangle are (3, 5), (7, 5) and (3, 9). What are the coordinates of the 4th vertex?

2. Plot these coordinates: (2, 6) (1, 5) (3, 5) (1, 3) (3, 3) (2, 2). What is the shape?

3. The points (−1, 1), (3, 5) and (−1, 5) are three of the four vertices of a square. What are the coordinates of the 4th vertex?

4. Draw a scalene triangle with each vertex in the second quadrant. Reflect the shape in the y axis and name the coordinates of each shape.

5. What shape is this? (−2, 6) (−2, 0) (−4, −4) (0, 4)

6. Name this shape: (3, −6) (−2, −1) (−2, 4) (3, −1)

Gold

a) Draw these problems in four quadrants to help you get the answers.

1. Join these points to make a straight line: (−4, 4) and (−4, −2). Write the coordinates of two different points that you could join to make a parallel line.

2. Draw these two lines: (4, 2) (6, −4) and (8, 2) (2, −4). Write the coordinates where they intersect.

3. These three points lie in a straight line. Name three other points on this line: (−4, 6) (0, 2) (−5, 7).

b) Copy these shapes and then rotate them (clockwise) by the amount shown. Sketch the result and write the coordinates.

1. Rotate by 90 degrees.

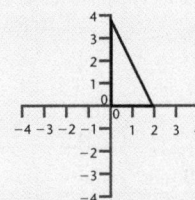

2. Rotate by 180 degrees.

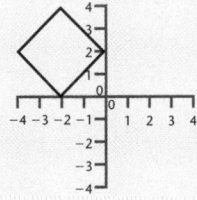

Training Tips

- The coordinates plot where the grid lines cross, not the space in between them.

37

SHAPE, SPACE AND MEASURES

Angles

An angle less than 90 degrees is acute.

A right angle is 90 degrees.

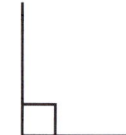

An angle greater than 90 degrees and less than 180 degrees is obtuse.

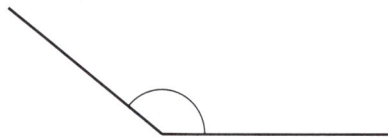

A reflex angle is greater than 180 degrees but less than 360 degrees.

An angle of 180 degrees is a straight line.

a) Estimate these angles:

1.

2.

3.

4.

b) Measure these angles:

1.

2.

3.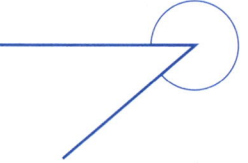

4.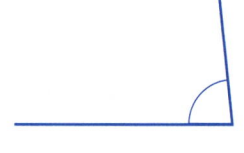

SHAPE, SPACE AND MEASURES

Silver

a) Estimate and then measure these angles:

1.

2.

3.

4.

5.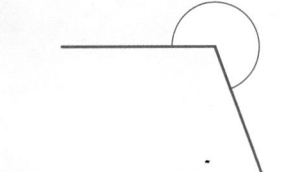

b) Draw these angles:

1. 63°   2. 166°   3. 245°
4. 15°   5. 229°

Training Tips
- The sum of all three angles inside a triangle is **180** degrees.
- There are **360** degrees in a complete rotation.

Gold

a) Estimate and then measure these angles to the nearest degree:

1.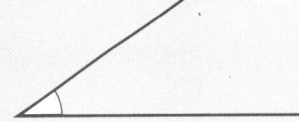

2.

3.

4.

5.

b) Draw these angles:

1. 179 degrees
2. 42 degrees
3. 86 degrees
4. 256 degrees
5. 345 degrees

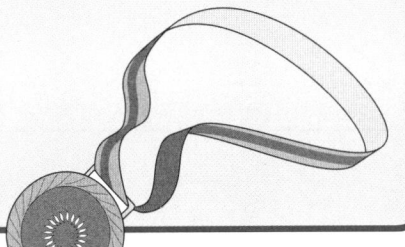

SHAPE, SPACE AND MEASURES

Angles in circles, triangles and straight lines

The total angles in a circle is 2 × 180° = 360°

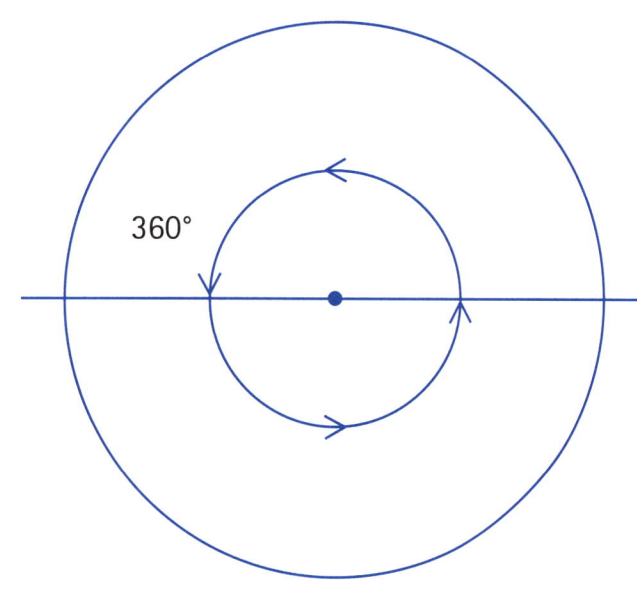

The angles within a triangle always equal 180°.

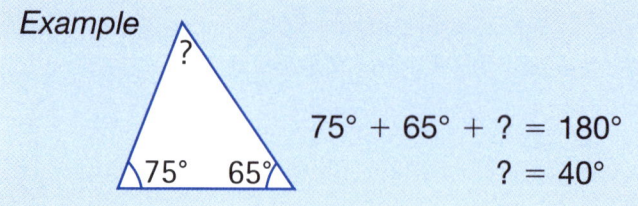

Any angles on a straight line add up to 180°.

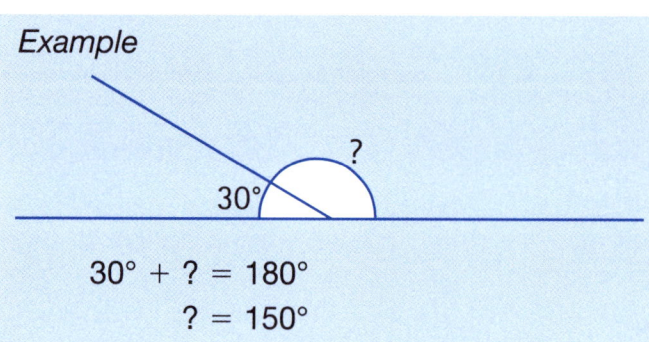

Bronze

a) Using the facts you have learnt, work out the missing angles:

1.

2.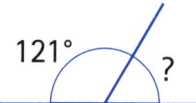

3.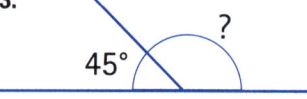

4.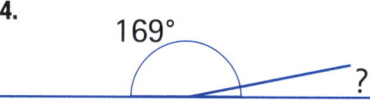

5.

Training Tips

- 180 degrees = a straight line or a half turn.
- 360 degrees = a circle or a whole turn.

b) Now work out these:

1.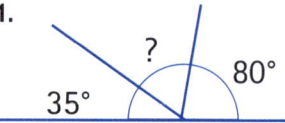

2.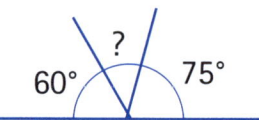

3.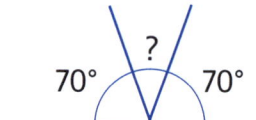

SHAPE, SPACE AND MEASURES

a) Find the missing angles:

1.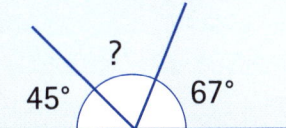

2.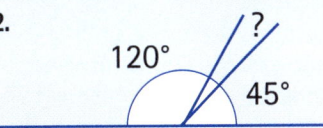

3.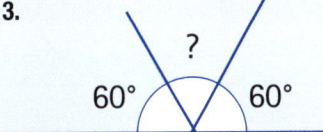

b) Find the missing angles:

1.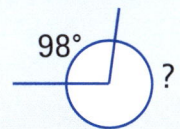

2.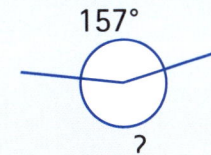

3.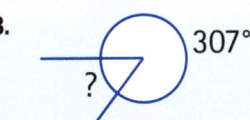

c) Find the missing angles:

1.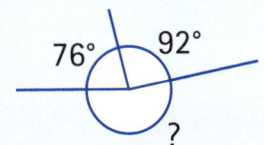

2.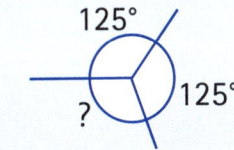

3.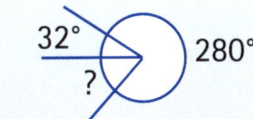

a) Find the missing angles:

1.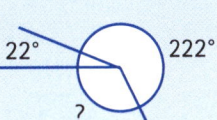

2.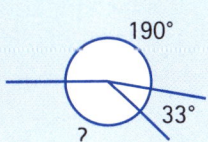

3.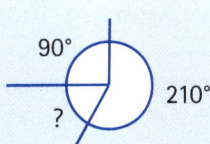

4.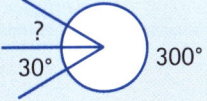

b) Find the missing angles:

1.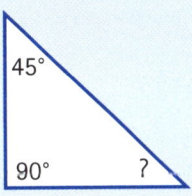

2.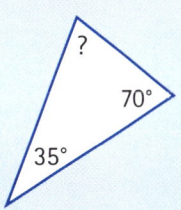

3.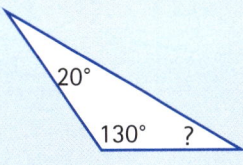

c) Now find these angles:

1.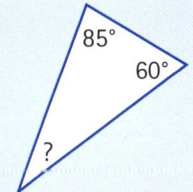

2.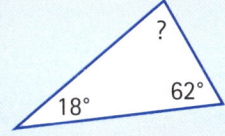

3.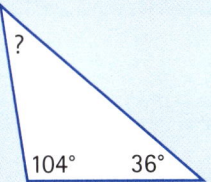

41

SOLVING PROBLEMS

Multi-step problems

These questions require you to perform two, three or maybe four steps in order to get them right!

1. Grant and Phil are selling penny sweets. They started with 1900. Grant sells 365 and Phil sells 773. How many sweets are left?

2. Jack and Joanna are selling clothes from a market stall. Jack sells £87 worth and Joanna sells £104 worth. They spend £50 on new stock. How much profit have they made?

3. Jenny buys 6 strips of raffle tickets and Jessica buys 5 strips. The raffle tickets cost 75p a strip. How much do they spend on raffle tickets altogether?

4. Stanley has read 156 of the 620 pages of his book 'Ten Thousand Miles in the Saddle' (by Ivor Rawbottom). How many more pages must Stanley read to reach the middle?

These questions require you to perform two, three or maybe four steps in order to get them right!

1. Louise has been given 100 football stickers. She gives a fifth of them to Hannah, a quarter of the remainder to Ryan and 26 to Jamie. How many stickers does Louise have left?

2. Ali bought three CDs for £15.99 each. His brother bought another two CDs at £13.99 each. How much did they spend together?

3. Each week Kim saves $\frac{1}{2}$ of her pocket money for a DVD player. If it takes her 30 weeks to save the £75 she needs for the player, how much is her pocket money per week?

4. There are 96 pages in this book. If there is an average of 45 questions on each page, how many questions do you need to complete to do half the book?

These questions require you to perform two, three or maybe four steps in order to get them right!

Use a calculator and your rounding skills for these questions.

Rising Stars Bank Interest Rates on Savings:	
£0–100	5% per annum
£101–£500	6% per annum
£501+	7% per annum

1. Sanjay saves £90 in his first year and makes £4.50 interest. In the second year he saves a further £200. What is the total in his account at the end of the second year?

2. Sanjay has £600 in the bank at the top rate of interest, how much will the account be worth in 2 years time?

3. If Sanjay takes £40 out of his account leaving £560, how much will the account be worth over the same 2 years?

4. If Sanjay saves for 5 years he gets a bonus payment of 10% of the final balance. If he saves £560 for 5 years, what is his final balance?

5. Sanjay's younger sister puts £1 into a Rising Stars bank account. If she leaves it there, how much will she have after 5 years? (Don't forget the bonus payment!)

- Once you have established the numbers you are calculating, estimate an answer of the calculation.

SOLVING PROBLEMS

Shopping problems

Solve these problems which are all about money and shopping bills. Learning to handle and deal with money is a very useful life-skill.

1. Find the total of these bills from the baker's shop – 76p, 93p, 58p and £4.75.
2. Petrol costs 72.6p per litre. How much does it cost to fill the tank of a scooter which holds 10 litres?

Supermarket prices	
Soap	£0.76p
Butter	£1.25
Chicken	£4.55
Soup	£0.54p
Carrots (500 g)	£2.24
Tomatoes (500 g)	£1.89
Apple juice (1 l)	£0.74p
Orange juice (1 l)	£1.01p

3. How much does soup, chicken and two litres of orange juice cost?
4. If Calum buys two bars of soap and a bag of carrots, how much does he need to spend?
5. Calum gives the shop assistant a £10 note. How much change should he get?
6. Maggie has £5.00 and buys a carton of apple juice, a packet of butter and a tin of tomatoes. How much change should she get?

Solve these problems which are all about money and shopping bills. Learning to handle and deal with money is a very useful life-skill.

1. What change from £50 would you get if you bought a football shirt for £29.99, some shorts for £9.99 and some socks for £5.99?
2. You can buy 5 cans of 'Burpsi' for £1.85. How much does one can cost?
3. Jeff has £100. He spends £24.50 on a necklace for his girlfriend, £41.78 on a meal for two and gives £12 to his younger brother for babysitting. How much does Jeff have left?

Txt Fun

Text message prices
First 500 messages 3p each
Next 500 messages 2.5p each
Further messages 2p each

4. James only sends 583 messages. How much is his bill?
5. Katy sends 1029 messages. How much does she spend?
6. Use the prices above. If all the children's messages were sent from one phone, what would the cost be?

Solve these problems which are all about money and shopping bills. Learning to handle and deal with money is a very useful life-skill.

1. What is the total of these supermarket bills? £104.52, £178.23, £42.89 and £29.91.
2. A burger van sells 4925 burgers at £1.35 each. What is the total cost of the burgers?

Melissa goes shopping with a £50 note and a £20 note. In the first shop she spends £12.56 on a DVD, £10.99 on a book and £9.98 on a CD. In the second shop she buys a pair of shoes for £17.99 and some shoe polish for £2.50.

3. How much change would she get from the £50 note?
4. How much does she spend in the second shop?
5. If she spends the £20 note in the second shop, how much change will she get?
6. Investigate the different notes and coins that Melissa might be left with at the end of her shopping trip.

- Scan the questions for important words and phrases such as 'How many' or 'Who' and 'What'.

43

SOLVING PROBLEMS

Converting foreign currency

If you go abroad you will probably have to change your money into a different currency. This can be confusing! How do you know how much you have and what you are spending?

Bronze

Look at this exchange rate at the bank.

£1 = 1.7 US Dollars
    2.4 Australian Dollars
    10.6 South African Rand
    184 Japanese Yen

1. How many US Dollars can I have for £2?

2. How many Australian Dollars can I have for £4?

3. How many Yen are there in £27.50?

4. I have 106 Rand. How much is this worth in pounds?

5. If I take £100 spending money on holiday to Florida, how many dollars will I have?

6. I send £50 to my aunt in Australia. How many dollars can she exchange it for?

7. Which is worth the most in pounds? A hundred Rand or a hundred US Dollars?

8. How many Yen can I have for £1000?

9. How many Yen is 25p worth?

10. What is the cost in US Dollars of a new computer costing £600?

Training Tips
- Foreign exchange rates change daily. Find out how much a Euro is worth today. Look in a newspaper or on the Internet.
- 1.35 Euros *to* a pound means that one pound *is worth* or is *the same as* 1.35 Euros.

SOLVING PROBLEMS

Silver

There are 1.35 Euros to £1.

1. What is the price in pounds of a car costing 15 400 Euros?
2. What is the price in Euros of a Plasma screen TV costing £3500?
3. If I have 1350 Euros, how much is this worth in pounds?
4. If I take £550 to spend in Italy, how many Euros will I exchange it for?
5. John pays 28 000 Euros for a new car in France. How many pounds would it have cost in England?

Use a calculator or a written method for these.

There are 85 Indian Rupees to £1

There are 96 Jamaican Dollars to £1

6. Find the price in Rupees of a house costing £105 000.
7. Find the price in Jamaican Dollars of a house costing £129 000.
8. Find the price in Rupees of a car costing £19 999.
9. How many Jamaican Dollars does a new motorbike cost if it is priced at £1750?
10. Which costs more in pounds and by how much – a DVD costing 850 rupees or a CD costing 864 Jamaican Dollars?

Gold

There are 1818 South Korean Won to £1.

1. If you had 1 818 000 Won, how many pounds would that be?
2. A flat costs £89 000. How much is that in South Korean Won?
3. Frankie earns £27 500 in a year. How much is that in Won?
4. How many Won is 1p worth?
5. Juan wins 100 000 Won on one wonderful game of one-on-one basketball. How many pounds has Juan won?

In Cyprus there are 0.77 Cypriot pounds to £1.

6. A bike costs £99. How much is that in Cypriot pounds?
7. A games console costs 120 Cypriot pounds. How much is that in £?
8. How many Cypriot pounds is Ali's £50 savings worth?
9. Layla earns 436 Cypriot pounds in her delicatessen. How much is that worth in pounds sterling?
10. Cem finds £2.50 in his pocket. How much is that in Cypriot pounds?

SOLVING PROBLEMS

Calculating fractions and percentages

Remember your fraction/percentage equivalents (see page 14). They will help you answer these questions.

a) There is a 10% discount at the sports shop. How much is the discount on these?

1. A £200 set of golf clubs
2. A £25 tennis racket
3. A £66 pair of trainers
4. A £48 cricket bat
5. A £110 croquet set

b) The agent's fee for securing sponsorship deals for a top footballer is 5%. Calculate the fee on these deals:

1. A £70 000 boot deal
2. A £120 000 shirt endorsement
3. £68 000 for promoting aftershave
4. A £83 000 mobile phone promotion
5. A £180 000 launch of a new range of underpants

c) When a player is sold an agent can get up to 20% of the transfer fee. Calculate the fees on these deals:

1. 7% of £150 000
2. 10% of £1 000 500
3. 15% of £3 333 333
4. 17.5% of £8 567 000
5. 20% of £18 350 235

Training Tips

- To find 0.5% – first find 10% then 10% of that and then halve your answer.
  e.g 0.5% of £60 = £6 then 60p then 30p

SOLVING PROBLEMS

 Silver

1. Work out how much I save if I buy a £6 pair of shorts at 10% discount.

2. How much would I save on a football if the price drops by 10% from £9.00?

3. The deposit on a £260 rowing machine is 50%. How much is the deposit?

4. There is a 'buy one get one half price' promotion on hockey sticks. The sticks are £8. If I buy two, how much will I spend?

5. The sports shop has an 'everything for half price' day. How much is a snooker cue sold for on half price day if it normally sells for £39.98?

6. A tennis racket is reduced by 10% from its original price of £22. What is the new price of the tennis racket?

7. Footballs have increased in price by 10% after the cup final. How much would a football cost that used to be £9.00?

8. A new track-suit costs £36. There is 25% off in the sale. How much does it cost now?

9. Tennis balls are £5 for 4 with a 15% reduction in the sale. What is the sale price of 4 tennis balls?

10. Socks are 20% off for a week. How much do 3 pairs cost in the sale if they are normally £5.00?

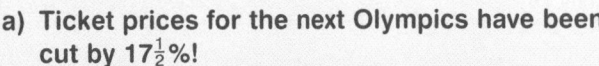 Gold

a) Ticket prices for the next Olympics have been cut by $17\frac{1}{2}$%!

   How much will these seats cost now?

   1. Upper tier block 34 – £35
   2. Lower tier block 4 – £55
   3. Track-side – £110
   4. Upper box – £125
   5. Lower box – £225

b) The agent's fee for negotiating sponsorship has now gone up to $12\frac{1}{2}$%!

   What are the fees for these deals?

   1. Promoting a sport drink – £25 000
   2. Modelling underpants – £45 000
   3. Appearing on the cover of FIFA 2006 video game – £95 000
   4. Selling small French cars on TV – £250 000
   5. Promoting bad eating habits with McChubbies burgers – £500 000

c) Work out the final price of these items, including the percentage increase or decrease:

   1. A sports drink at £1.99 reduced by 15%
   2. A football at £9.99 increased by 25%
   3. A pair of socks at £4.99 reduced by 8%
   4. A tracksuit at £15.99 reduced by 12%
   5. A pair of boots at £25.99 increased by 17.5%

47

Problems involving length

These are 'story' problems involving kilometres, metres, centimetres and millimetres.
Remember which units the questions are using (km, m, cm, mm).

1. James jumped 145 cm in the long jump. Carl's final jump was 4 cm less. How far did Carl jump?

2. Priya ran 1200 m. Stephen ran $\frac{1}{2}$ as far. How far did he run?

3. Dave runs 12 times around the track to raise money for his school. Once around the track is 400 m. How many metres does Dave run in total?

4. Carl jumped 138 cm and 127 cm in the long jump. How far did he jump in metres altogether?

5. Sasha threw the javelin 63 cm further than Sabrina who threw it 12.25 m. How far did Sasha throw the javelin?

6. Cathy jumps 113 cm in the high jump. That is 40 mm more than Jessie. How high in cm does Jessie jump?

7. Zoe ran three and a half times further than Claire who ran 1500 m. How far did Zoe run?

8. Mr Quick the PE teacher could do the 100 m in 25 seconds but Stephanie was 50% quicker. How long did it take Stephanie to run the 100 m?

9. Erin has run $\frac{1}{4}$ of a 200 m race. How far has she still got to run?

10. Meena threw the javelin 10 m. Jane threw it 10% less. How far did Jane throw the javelin?

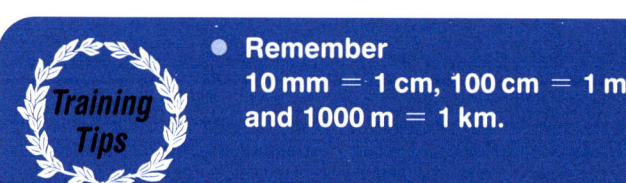

- Remember
10 mm = 1 cm, 100 cm = 1 m and 1000 m = 1 km.

SOLVING PROBLEMS

Silver

These are 'story' problems involving kilometres, metres, centimetres and millimetres.
Remember which units the questions are using (km, m, cm, mm).

1. In the 10 000 m race, Harpreet has run 5 laps of 400 m. How many metres has Harpreet still got to run?

2. Greg has completed $\frac{3}{4}$ of the 20 km cycle race. How many metres has he left to go?

3. How many centimetres are covered from start to finish by eight athletes running the 100 m?

4. Leo jumped 1.98 m, Finley jumped 2.79 m and Jamie jumped 63 cm less than Finley. What is the total distance of all three long jumps?

5. Wesley threw a cricket ball 720 mm further than Joseph who threw it 58.23 m. How many metres did Wesley throw the cricket ball?

6. Jason threw the cricket ball 1215 mm past the end of the tape measure. If the tape measure was 60 m, how far did Jason throw the cricket ball?

7. Sofie has run 25% of the 800 m race. How far has she got to go?

8. Finn has run the 100 m, 200 m and 400 m. How many centimetres has he run so far?

9. If Finn now runs the 1500 m, how many centimetres will he have run in total?

10. Lloyd jumped 2.04 m, then 1.85 m and then 1.92 m. What is the distance between his longest and shortest jumps?

Gold

These are 'story' problems involving kilometres, metres, centimetres and millimetres.
Remember which units the questions are using (km, m, cm, mm).

1. Lyndsey jumped 6 mm further than Alice who jumped 7.5 cm less than Jenny. Jenny jumped 1.45 m. How far did Lyndsey jump?

2. How many millimetres does an athlete run if they complete the 10 000 m?

3. How many centimetres do all 8 teams cover when they race the 4 × 100 m relay?

4. How many centimetres do all 8 teams cover when they race the 4 × 400 m relay?

5. The distances for 4 javelin throws were as follows: 45.36 m, 73.51 m, 78.77 m and 72.62 m. What was the total distance in centimetres?

6. Kofi has run 18% of the 400 m race. How far has he got to go now?

7. The high jump was won by Joanne with a jump of 1.56 m. The second place jump was 32 mm less. How high did the second jumper jump?

8. Jack ran in the 800 m, the 1500 m and the 10 000 m. How many kilometres did he run?

9. Rachel threw the javelin 40 metres. If Sam threw the javelin 6.34 m less than Rachel but the same as Peter who threw it 38.35 m, how far was Rachel's throw?

10. Ben didn't finish any of his races but ran 30% of the 100 m, 25% of the 400 m and $\frac{1}{5}$ of the 1500 m. How far did he run in total?

SOLVING PROBLEMS

Problems involving mass

Bronze

These are 'story' problems involving kilograms (kg) and grams (g).

1. A weightlifter lifts 48 kg more than his opponent who lifts 165 kg. How much does the weightlifter lift?

2. David lifts 6500 g more than Martin who lifts 170 kg. How many kg does David lift?

3. My sports bag weighs 2 kg. If I take out my running shoes it weighs 400 g less. How much does my sports bag weigh now?

4. Martin lifts 173 kg and David lifts 31 kg more. How many kg does David lift?

5. Martin trains hard for a month. He lifts 210 kg! David lifts 920 g less. How many kg does David lift now?

Silver

These are 'story' problems involving kilograms (kg) and grams (g).

1. The wrestler 'Puny Pete' is 300 g heavier than 'Nerdy Nigel' who is 48.90 kg. How heavy is 'Puny Pete' in kg?

2. Steve's football boots weigh 760 g each. How much do the two boots weigh together?

3. James has 2.56 kg of sweets to sell. If he manages to get rid of 1.02 kg of sweets, how much is left?

4. How many grams of horse feed must be added to 2.73 kg to make 5 kg of horse feed altogether?

5. How many grams of sugar will I need to make a sugar smoothie for 8 people if one smoothie requires 45 grams?

Gold

These are 'story' problems involving kilograms (kg) and grams (g).

1. What is the difference in grams between a bike that weighs 11.78 kg and a cyclist that weighs 73.9 kg?

2. What is the difference in kg between a boxer who weighs 91 585 g and one who weighs 89.6 kg?

3. Johnny weighs 73.451 kg and Alex weighs 62.1 kg. What is the difference in grams?

4. Bruce the potter has a lump of clay that weighs 309 kg. Each pot that Bruce makes needs 120 g of clay. How many pots can Bruce make from his lump of clay?

5. Brian the builder has 3.69 kg of nails in his toolbox. If he uses 35 nails and has 0.54 kg of nails left, how much does each nail weigh?

- Adding the zero to decimal numbers can help when you are dealing with numbers to 3 decimal places, e.g. 56.4 kg is actually 56 kg and 400 g.

SOLVING PROBLEMS

Problems involving capacity

Bronze

These are 'story' problems involving litres (l), millilitres (ml) and centilitres (cl).

1. A runner drinks 345 ml of water straight after a race and another 470 ml a little later. How many ml of water has the runner drunk altogether?

2. A car holds 50 litres of petrol. A van holds three and a half times as much. How many litres of petrol can the van hold?

3. How many 250 ml jugs of water are needed to fill a bowl which holds 6 litres?

4. If Peter has a bottle of drink which contains 330 cl, how many centilitres will he have left if he drinks 175 cl?

5. How many litres of juice are there in 6 cartons – with each carton containing 500 ml?

Silver

These are 'story' problems involving litres (l), millilitres (ml) and centilitres (cl).

1. Wendy uses 25 oranges to make $1\frac{1}{4}$ litres of orange juice. How many litres of orange juice can she make with 75 oranges?

2. A container full of orange juice holds 4.2 litres. A full jug holds 200 ml of orange juice. How many full jugs will it take to fill the container?

3. A container which holds 7.8 litres of cola is knocked over. 1.9 litres is spilt. How many litres of cola are left in the container?

4. Kerry has 6 cups of tea each day. Each cup holds 275 ml of tea. How much tea does Kerry drink each day?

5. Charlie has 20 000 cl of water in his garden pond. How many litres is that?

Gold

These are 'story' problems involving litres (l), millilitres (ml) and centilitres (cl).

1. A drinks stand sells 623 cans of 'Burpsi' in a day. Each can holds 330 ml. How many litres of Burpsi are sold?

2. If the stand sells 5000 cans containing 330 ml of Burpsi in a week, how many litres is that?

3. A supermarket sells 6241 pots of fresh soup in a week. Each pot contains 750 ml. How many litres of soup is that?

4. The least popular soup in the supermarket is 'Offal Broth' which sells 26 pots of 750 ml each week. The most popular soup is 'Cream of Chocolate' which sells 4,396 pots of 750 ml. What is the difference in litres?

5. A lorry which delivers soup holds 7000 pots, each pot containing 50 ml. However, the lorry overturns on the motorway and 5113 pots of soup are smashed (causing a 'souper' explosion!). How many litres of soup are left?

Training Tips
- Remember — 10 ml = 1 cl
  1000 ml = 1 litre
  100 cl = 1 litre

51

SOLVING PROBLEMS

Problems involving imperial measures

The Imperial system is the old system of measurement. We mainly use the metric system but it is very useful to be able to convert units of one system to the units of the other.

Use this conversion table to help you answer these questions.

Imperial to Metric	Metric to Imperial
1 mile = 1.61 km	1 km = 0.62 mile
1 yard (36 inches) = 91.4 cm	1 m = 39 inches
1 foot = 30.5 cm	1 cm = 0.39 inch
1 inch = 2.54 cm	1 l = 1.76 pts
1 gallon = 4.55 l	1 g = 0.04 oz
1 pint = 0.57 l	1 kg = 2.20 lb
1 pound = 0.45 kg	
1 ounce = 28.35 g	

1. How long in centimetres is a 10 inch photo-frame?
2. How heavy in pounds is a suitcase weighing 5 kg?
3. How many litres of petrol are there in a tank which contains 10 gallons?
4. How many yards are there in 400 metres?
5. How many pints are there in 10 litres?
6. What is 12 feet in metres?
7. If I run 2.5 miles, how many kilometres is that?
8. My book weighs about 250 g. How many ounces is that?

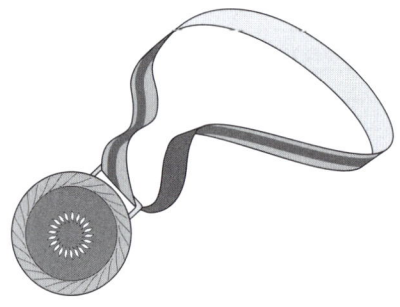

- Most distances on road signs in the United Kingdom are measured in miles. Next time you are on a car journey, see if you can convert a road sign into kilometres.

SOLVING PROBLEMS

1. How many centimetres does Jimmy win the race by if he wins by a yard?

2. The 1500 m race is run over how many yards?

3. The 5000 m race is run over how many yards?

4. My Dad is 5 feet and 10 inches tall. How tall is this in centimetres?

5. My Dad weighs 12 stone. How heavy is this in kilograms and grams?

Pancake Ingredients
100 g flour
200 ml milk
100 ml water
1 egg
50 g butter

6. How many ounces of flour do I need to make these pancakes?

7. How much liquid am I adding to the flour, in pints?

8. Do I need more or less than 2 ounces of butter for this recipe?

1. A champion javelin thrower throws the javelin 90 m. How many inches is that?

2. Mount Everest is 29 028 feet tall. How tall is this to the nearest metre?

3. The River Nile is the longest river in the world. It stretches 3900 miles. How far is this in kilometres?

4. How far is this in yards?

5. How far is this in inches?

Scone Ingredients
(makes 10 scones)
250 g flour
50 g caster sugar
125 ml milk

6. How many ounces of dry ingredients will I need to make this recipe?

7. My mixing jug is only in Imperial measures. How many pints of milk will I need?

8. I want to make the mixture sweeter. If I add another ounce of sugar, how many ounces will there be in total?

53

SOLVING PROBLEMS

Problems involving time

These 'story' problems are about time. 'Counting on' can be a useful way of solving them.

1. The women's marathon started at 08:30 and finished at 10:57. How long did the race last?

2. The men's marathon started at 12:55 and lasted for 2 hours and eight minutes. At what time did it finish?

3. Four runners in the school 4 x 400 m relay run the following times: 84.2 seconds, 89.5 seconds, 93.7 seconds and 77.7 seconds. What is the total time in minutes for all four runners?

4. Mike ran the 100 m in 13.63 seconds. Neil came second and was 1.72 seconds slower. What was Neil's time for the 100 m?

5. Diane swam 200 m in 7 minutes and 25 seconds. She swam a further 300 m in 10 minutes and 56 seconds. What was her total time taken to swim 500 m?

6. Next year's sports day will take place 362 days after this year's. If this year's sports day took place on 5th July, what day will next year's be on? Next year is not a leap year.

7. The Olympics takes place over 28 days. If it starts on the 28th of July, when will it end?

8. The longest marathon was run by Lloyd Scott (in a diving costume). It took him six days, four hours, 30 minutes and 56 seconds to complete the Edinburgh Marathon in 2003. How long is this in hours?

Training Tips

- 60 seconds = 1 minute
- 24 hours = 1 day
- 52 weeks = 1 year

60 minutes = 1 hour
7 days = 1 week
12 months = 1 year   10 years = a decade

SOLVING PROBLEMS

Silver

This is a table showing the cooking times for different types of meat.

Copy and complete the table.

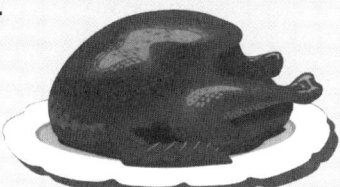

Kilograms/Cooking Times	1 kg	1.5 kg	2 kg	2.5 kg	3 kg	3.5 kg
Chicken (45 mins per kg + 20 mins)						
Beef (55 mins per kg + 20 mins)						
Pork (66 mins per kg + 35 mins)						
Lamb (50 mins per kg + 25 mins)						

Gold

1. The runner Paula Radcliffe's birthday is on December 17th. How many days ago was it from today?

2. How many months have you been alive?

3. How many weeks have you been alive?

4. How many days have you been alive?

5. How many weeks until your 100th birthday?

How many seconds:

6. In a football match?

7. In a week?

8. Do you spend at school each day?

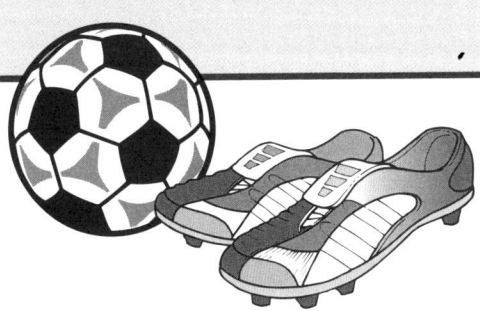

HANDLING DATA

Frequency bar charts

Graphs are an excellent way to show what data looks like. Bar charts or bar line charts are easier to read than looking at lots of numbers.

This frequency bar chart shows the number of pets owned by the children in a Year 6 Class.

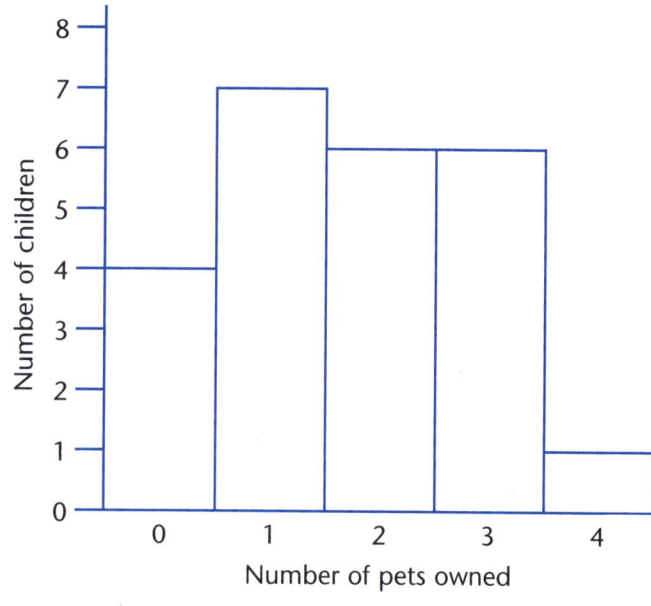

1. How many children owned one pet?
2. How many children owned three pets?
3. How many children owned two or more pets?
4. How many children owned less than two pets?
5. How many children are there in the Year 6 class?
6. What was the most number of pets owned by any of the children?
7. What was the most common (mode) number of pets owned?

Training Tips

- Think clearly and work step by step.

56

HANDLING DATA

Frequency charts may have grouped data. This makes the data easier to handle.

Silver

Here is a frequency bar chart showing the number of questions answered correctly in the school 'Pop Quiz'.

1. How many children scored between 11 and 15 marks?
2. How many children scored between 0 and 5 marks?
3. How many children scored more than 20 marks?
4. How many children scored more than 10 marks?
5. How many children scored less than 11 marks?
6. What was the most common score in the pop quiz?
7. What was the maximum number of marks you could score?

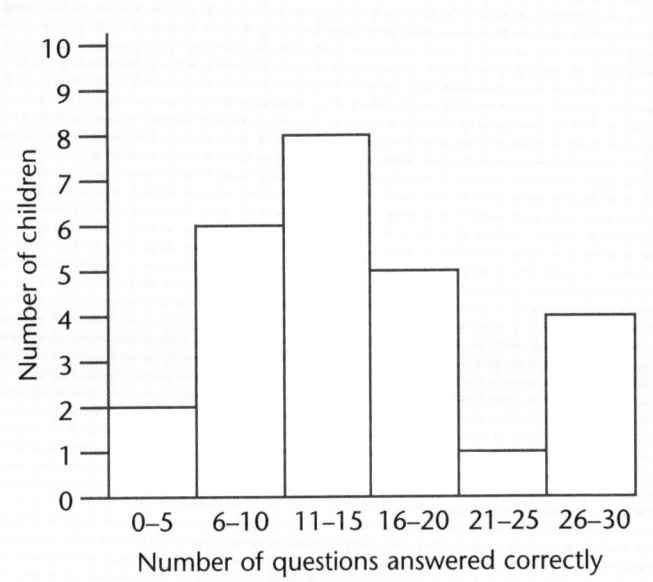

Gold

Look at the frequency bar chart in the Silver Medal question above. The children did the same quiz again a week later during a wet lunchtime.

Their scores improved! Here are their scores.

Group the data in the same way and redraw the bar chart. What differences do you notice between the two charts?

Amy – 29	Jamal – 26	Sally – 25
Benny –27	Kirsty – 18	Tyrone – 13
Callum – 19	Logan – 30	Una – 8
Deniece – 20	Mimi – 28	Vinny – 6
Elizabeth – 22	Nell – 10	Will – 23
Fran – 14	Oprah – 11	Xavier – 11
Gareth – 9	Pierce – 17	Yunis – 24
Harry – 21	Quentin – 1	Zachary – 29
Isobelle – 21	Ricardo – 25	

57

HANDLING DATA

Line graphs

A graph with time on the x axis and numbers on the y axis is often shown with a line. Sometimes the graph will show a set of points joined together by a line.
This shows how something is changing over a period of time.

This line graph shows the monthly sales of 'Spray-Rider' surf boards.

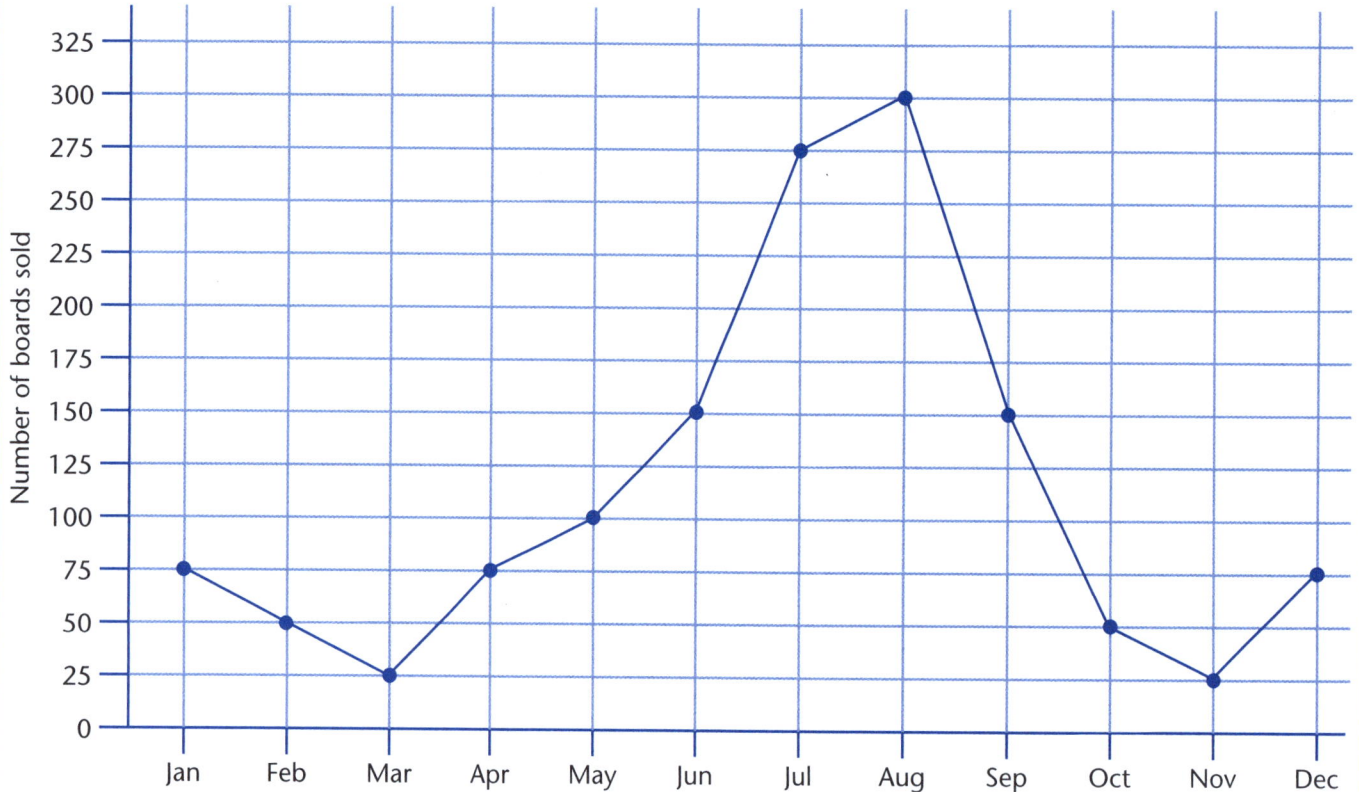

1. In which month were most boards sold?
2. How many surf boards were sold in April?
3. Between which two months did sales first start to rise?
4. Which month do you think Spray-Rider boards were offered with a 75% discount?
5. How many more boards were sold in September than December?
6. Why might there have been more sales in December than November?

• When reading graphs, go **up** from the x axis first to meet the line, and then read **across** from the y axis to read the **value**.

58

HANDLING DATA

Silver

This line graph is useful for converting miles to kilometres and vice versa.

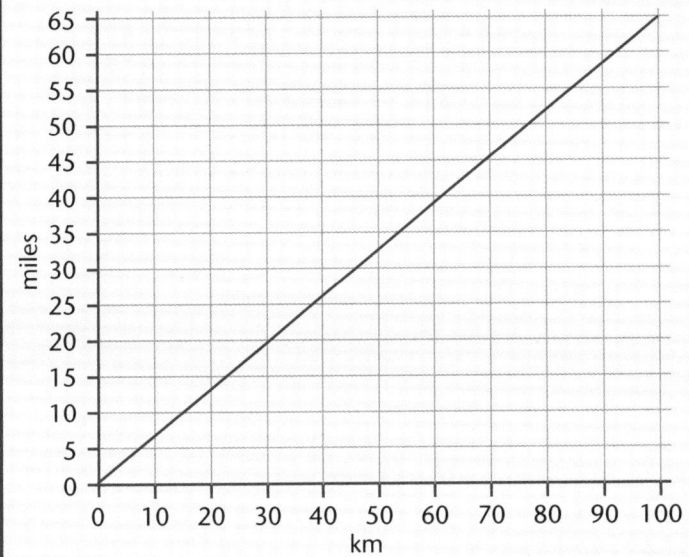

Using the line graph, change these road signs from km to miles or miles to km.

1.
Brighton	20 miles
Lewes	15 miles
Eastbourne	5 miles

2.
Bromley	35 miles
Central London	25 miles
Ashford	15 miles

3.
Manchester	40 km
Worsley	35 km
Chadderton	20 km

4.
Newcastle	50 km
Sunderland	18 km
Durham	4 km

Gold

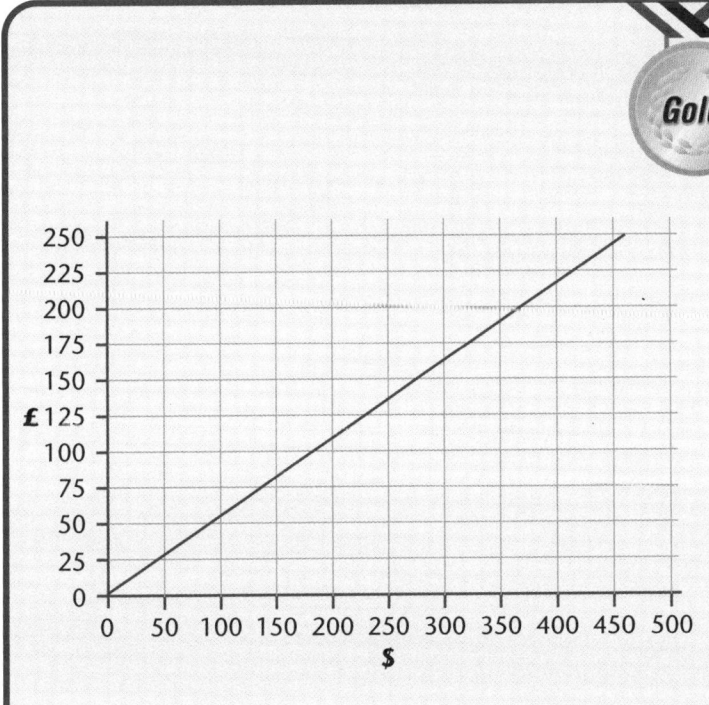

The tourist rate for the USA is one pound to $1.85.

1. The Osborne family go on holiday to Wild World in Florida. They take £250 spending money. How many Dollars can they exchange that for?

2. Jack takes £80. How many Dollars can he exchange it for?

3. Kelly exchanges £120 for Dollars but only spends a third of them. How many pounds does she have after converting back her Dollars?

4. Jack is confused! He now has £30 in pounds and $30 in dollars. How much does he have altogether in pounds?

HANDLING DATA

Probability

Probability is all about how likely something is to happen.
There are different ways of showing this.

a) Match one of these words to each of the statements below.

CERTAIN   LIKELY   UNLIKELY   IMPOSSIBLE

1. The next Olympics will be held in July 1967.
2. The sun will rise tomorrow.
3. Next Easter will be in April.
4. Tomorrow I will go outside during breaktime.
5. I will sit at the same table in class tomorrow.
6. Great Britain will win a medal at the next Olympics.
7. It will snow next Valentine's day.

b) Draw this probability line in your book.
Place these statements where you think they should appear on the line.

1. I will grow an extra head before bedtime.
2. Henry VIII will take part in 'Big Brother'.
3. The sun will set this evening.
4. There will be snow next Christmas.
5. Great Britain will win 50 Gold Medals at the next Olympics.
6. I will go outside next Saturday.
7. If I throw a dice it will land on an even number.

• However many times you toss a coin, there is still an even chance of getting tails.

HANDLING DATA

Silver

Draw this probability scale in your book.

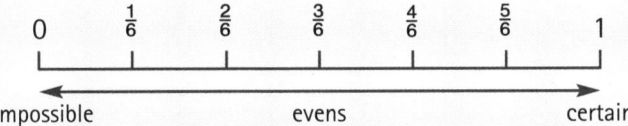

a) Charlie is rolling a 1 to 6 dice. Place each of these events on the scale using an arrow.

1. Charlie rolls an odd number.
2. Charlie rolls a number greater than 4.
3. He rolls a 7.
4. He rolls a 6.

b) There are 24 beads placed in a bag. 8 are red, 4 are blue, 6 are green and the rest are yellow. Charlie picks a bead. Draw a probability scale in your book. Place these statements on the scale.

1. The next bead Charlie picks will be blue.
2. The next bead picked from the bag will be purple.
3. The next bead picked by Charlie will be yellow.

c) Charlie now gets rid of the yellow beads. What are the chances of these events happening? Use a fraction in your answer.

1. The next bead Charlie picks will be blue.
2. The next bead picked from the bag will be yellow.
3. The next bead picked by Charlie will be red.

Gold

impossible		even chance		certain
0%	25%	50%	75%	100%
0	0.25	0.5	0.75	1
0	$\frac{1}{4}$	$\frac{1}{2}$	$\frac{3}{4}$	1

Use the grid above to help you to answer these by writing a fraction, a decimal or a percentage. Remember the answers may be between those numbers in the grid!

1. I am thinking of a certain day of the week. What chance is there that you could guess the day I'm thinking of? Write your answer as a fraction.

2. I have 4 playing cards face down on a table. One of them is the ace of spades. What is the chance of you picking the ace of spades? Write your answer as a percentage.

3. There are 8 beads in a bag. Four are yellow, three are blue and one is red. What is the chance that I would pick out a blue bead? Write your answer as a fraction.

4. There are 10 cards on a table, four tens, four queens and two kings. What is the chance that you would pick a queen? Write your answer as a decimal.

5. A football match ends 1–0 after 90 minutes. What chance is there that the goal was scored between 50 and 55 minutes? Answer with a percentage.

HANDLING DATA

Finding the mean and the median

The **mean** is the average of a group of numbers. To find the mean – add all the amounts and divide by the number of amounts.

Example
19, 21, 23, 22, 24, 22, 23
Mean
= (19 + 21 + 23 + 22 + 24 + 22 + 23) ÷ 7
= 154 ÷ 7 = 22

The **median** is the middle number in a group of numbers. To find the median – put the numbers in order from smallest to largest and find the middle number.

Example
234, 345, 404, 222, 304, 411, 208
Median
= 208, 222, 234, 304, 345, 404, 411
= 304 (the middle number)

 Bronze

a) Find the mean of these sets of scores:
1. 11, 19, 20, 14, 18, 25, 26, 19, 19
2. 5, 16, 18, 20, 14, 11, 23, 16, 12
3. 32, 40, 39, 36, 38, 29, 31, 28, 33
4. 58, 55, 51, 48, 55, 48, 50, 51, 52

b) Find the median of these numbers:
1. 349, 330, 321, 333, 401, 379, 345
2. 789, 777, 703, 693, 715, 733, 736
3. 253, 255, 257, 238, 239, 244, 254
4. 218, 299, 204, 257, 259, 226, 245

 Silver

a) Find the mean of these sets of scores:
1. 121, 189, 184, 230, 164, 148, 215, 236, 169
2. 563, 416, 538, 480, 503, 434, 398, 546, 449
3. 732, 640, 568, 775, 652, 619, 756, 599, 662
4. 518, 515, 516, 517, 515, 518, 509, 514, 513

b) Find the median of these numbers:
1. 3490, 2330, 4301, 3578, 4008, 3278, 4113
2. 6783, 7977, 7603, 6953, 7815, 6733, 6736
3. 4203, 4456, 4702, 4103, 5541, 4491, 4493
4. 8019, 8434, 8839, 8644, 8593, 8238, 8426

 Gold

a) Find the mean of these sets of scores:
1. 970, 919, 904, 999, 954, 938, 993, 956, 953
2. 1393, 1334, 1367, 1388, 1321, 1357
3. 3732, 3240, 3567, 3379, 3210, 3422
4. 6102, 6220, 6266, 6319, 6442, 6247

b) Find the median of these numbers:
1. 8930, 8892, 8789, 8834, 8821
2. 9012, 9220, 9326, 9245, 9222
3. 11 011, 11 101, 11 111, 11 110, 11 012
4. 9999, 9989, 9909, 9899, 9809

 Training Tips

- Median is the middle (or medium) number.

HANDLING DATA

Finding the mode

The mode is the most common value in a group of numbers. To find the mode – sort the numbers into sets of the same amount. Look for the set with the most numbers.

Example
23, 24, 22, 25, 23, 21, 26, 21, 22, 23
Group the numbers

21 22 **23** 24 25 26
21 22 **23**
        23

23 is the mode of this set

Bronze

Find the mode of these sets of scores:

1. 32, 33, 34, 35, 32, 33, 32, 33, 32, 36, 36
2. 21, 20, 21, 19, 22, 20, 21, 19, 20, 21, 25
3. 45, 44, 43, 40, 40, 43, 44, 45, 43, 40, 43
4. 76, 75, 77, 75, 79, 75, 76, 75, 78, 75, 76
5. 55, 55, 55, 54, 53, 54, 53, 54, 54, 55, 54
6. 101, 110, 101, 111, 111, 100, 110, 101, 109
7. 210, 212, 210, 211, 211, 212, 213, 212, 213
8. 222, 202, 220, 210, 211, 202, 202, 211, 221

Silver

a) Find the mode of these sets of numbers:

1. 480, 481, 488, 481, 483, 483, 488, 480, 481, 482
2. 326, 335, 363, 330, 324, 326, 337, 338, 364, 331
3. 101, 111, 100, 101, 111, 101, 100, 110, 111, 101

b) Create a set of six numbers that could produce these modes. Try to make them really difficult to answer.

1. 68
2. 101
3. 989
4. 325

Gold

a) Find the mode of these sets of numbers:

1. 1, 1, 2, 2, 1, 2, 1, 2, 1, 2, 2, 1, 1, 2, 2
2. 3, 3, 4, 4, 5, 5, 3, 4, 5, 2, 4, 5, 3, 3, 2
3. 934, 923, 922, 934, 903, 933, 935, 923, 934, 993

b) Create a set of eight numbers that could produce these modes. Try to make them really difficult to answer.

1. 5
2. 110
3. 999
4. 10 001

- Mode is the Most Common Value.

HANDLING DATA

Finding the range

The range is the difference between the greatest and the least in a set of data. Here are the scores out of 100 for the contestants in an archery contest.

> 52, 77, 21, 44, 86, 86, 62, 39, 95
> The range is 74. (95 − 21 = 74)

Bronze

a) Find the range of these test results out of a hundred:

1. 76, 34, 78, 54, 25, 26, 28, 47, 46, 78, 88
2. 22, 56, 76, 88, 89, 99, 15, 33, 75, 59, 78
3. 45, 67, 89, 37, 76, 75, 77, 90, 64, 66, 63
4. 22, 26, 28, 19, 34, 67, 15, 77, 46, 54, 33

b) Find the range of these darts scores:

1. 120, 100, 101, 86, 50, 75, 65, 160, 39, 77
2. 177, 105, 115, 164, 146, 111, 180, 96, 102
3. 56, 65, 64, 67, 59, 112, 77, 106, 108, 82
4. 90, 96, 67, 71, 81, 120, 115, 164, 119, 80

Silver

a) Find the range of these computer game scores out of a thousand:

1. 849, 576, 386, 251, 693, 779
2. 624, 235, 907, 451, 356, 156
3. 354, 785, 651, 951, 357, 627
4. 156, 123, 145, 167, 841, 354

b) Now find the range of these scores:

1. 1250, 1425, 986, 674, 1402, 1328
2. 845, 867, 1249, 1167, 1346, 1406
3. 964, 1256, 826, 1460, 1239, 1488
4. 674, 539, 783, 485, 1351, 1029

Gold

a) Find the range of these theme park attendance figures:

1. 6783, 5493, 4463, 6745, 3459
2. 3267, 1567, 3654, 1289, 4587
3. 3265, 1266, 6537, 9514, 3647
4. 3645, 1259, 3665, 6034, 6154

b) Now find the range of these football attendances:

1. 9687, 8006, 6779, 7126, 7764
2. 9015, 6648, 7086, 7916, 9267
3. 9035, 8776, 6716, 6325, 8415
4. 6297, 9167, 9930, 8149, 8836

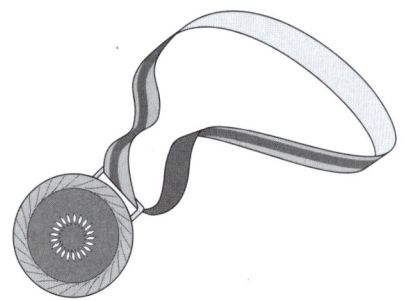

Training Tips

- It can help if you write the numbers down again in order of size.